# TWENTY-FIFTH ANNUAL
# HEDGE FUND
# CONFERENCE

May 22–24, 2022 | Miami Beach, FL

RITA KAKATI-SHAH

# THE GODDESS OF GO-GETTING

YOUR GUIDE TO CONFIDENCE,
LEADERSHIP, AND WORKPLACE SUCCESS

Tellwell Talent
www.tellwell.ca

ISBN
978-0-2288-7020-3 (Hardcover)
978-0-2288-7019-7 (Paperback)
978-0-2288-7021-0 (eBook)

RITA KAKATI-SHAH is a renowned thought leader who helps corporations attract, retain, and develop previously marginalized or overlooked pools of talented employees. As a successful finance professional Rita personally experienced what it was like to navigate the workforce as a woman of color. Her experiences in that area were helpful when she hit an equally pervasive obstacle: that of returning to paid work after raising her children.

As a result of hearing about similar experiences of other individuals who faced a variety of obstacles in returning to or thriving within the workplace, Rita developed Uma, an international strategic coaching, consulting, and training platform that empowers confidence, inspires success, and builds leadership and resilience in women and minorities through diversity, inclusion, and retention strategies.

Rita began to work with numerous groups of minority employees: returning veterans, mothers returning to paid work after having children, new fathers who struggled with taking paternity leaves, women looking to reach senior leadership, people of different races, life circumstances and backgrounds, including C-Suite men and senior leadership who just couldn't retain their employees—all of whom offered valuable skills to their workplace but often weren't able to contribute as best as they could due to lack of flexibility, confidence, perception, bias, or decency. Rita focuses her coaching and corporate training on building confidence and taking ownership, while learning how to communicate concisely, negotiate wisely, and thereby developing a strong sense of belonging.

It turns out that corporations recognize that more employees than not at some point in their lives face a life situation that requires a level of flexibility, understanding, and decency from their employer, and that employers who allow for such flexibility enjoy a strong, supportive workplace culture that allows corporations to best attract, retain, and develop new hires and current employees.

"Rita's passion to develop and empower women and minorities in the workplace shines through on every page. Packed full of tips and tactics from Rita's inspiring journey, this book is a fascinating read, and not to be missed!"
*– Professor Stephen Bach, Executive Dean, King's Business School, King's College London*

"In *The Goddess of Go-Getting*, Kakati-Shah has masterfully brought to life the multitude of challenges faced by vulnerable people, especially women. Without getting preachy, she proposes a direction for our society that is getting more and more diverse. It is a welcome attempt at deepening our inter-cultural conversation, something that we all can learn from."
*– Mr. Randhir Jaiswal, Consul General of India in New York*

"Rita's multicultural upbringing across borders and her professional background provide unique perspectives of how women can bring out their voice with confidence and build their professional pathways. Her book is as much philosophical as it is practical, and, more so, personal, and relatable. It provides diverse angles and approaches inspiring women to deconstruct, discover, and strengthen their self-awareness to embrace their inner goddess and become change agents."
*– Professor Marion Philadelphia, Marshall School of Business, University of Southern California*

"This book by the wonderful Rita is full of practical and purposeful advice on accountability, allyship, mentoring, and the critical steps to overcoming fears that we can all take (as leaders and colleagues) to hire, progress and retain great talent BECAUSE of our unique differences in age, sex, color, creed, plus physical and cognitive abilities – definitely worth a read!"
*– Harriet Green OBE, Global Business Leader and Former Chairman & CEO, IBM, Asia Pacific*

"Rita Kakati-Shah is a woman of the world but, more importantly, she is a woman of the people. This book is rare in its balance of the pragmatic tips and skills needed to succeed at work with the broader picture of why we need to rethink our approaches to advancement and inclusion. Rita's work celebrates diversity while offering the unique global lens of her life and work. She brings healthy doses of humanity and humor to the Uma approach, and her efficient prose and captivating storytelling leave you with so many applicable lessons from the ultimate goddess of go-getting herself."

*– S. Mitra Kalita, CEO, URL Media, Columnist, Time magazine author, Pulitzer Prize winner and former CNN, LA Times, Washington Post, Wall Street Journal*

"I thoroughly enjoyed reading Rita's book because it is authentic and written with honesty and integrity to a wide range of topics. Rita draws significant parallels between the importance of the school experiences we have, to becoming successful adults in both work and social circles. When Rita talks about the 'rules of the playground' she has managed to accurately capture the essence of developing social awareness and open-mindedness to 'play the game' in the right way to benefit yourself – Rita Kakati-Shah is certainly the Goddess of Go-Getting!"

*– Mark Roessler, School Principal, Ormiston Park Academy, London, England*

"In *The Goddess of Go-Getting*, Rita takes her personal and childhood anecdotes and fits them brilliantly to the corporate world, allowing us to learn and understand that our uniqueness and difference is what makes us stand out. Her amazing tips to strive in all phases of our lives are a treasure!"

*– Marium Abid, Brown Girl Magazine, UK*

"Rita Kakati-Shah navigates the reader through the complexities of diversity, inclusivity and related topics in THE GODDESS OF GO-GETTING, drawing upon her extensive experience in the corporate world and in life. The author immediately contextualizes her role from the outset, providing an overview of her background and current role. This establishes Kakati-Shah as a credible source of advice and information, as someone who has experienced and dealt with the range of issues she covers in her book. From being a young child, the author describes a sense of being 'different', a girl enjoying more boyish pastimes; later, she experiences the struggles of being an 'outsider', firstly as an ambitious female of color in the U.K. and then as a female in male-dominated work environments.

"Inspired by the fighting spirit of her immigrant parents, the author refuses to fall prey to victimhood. Resilience is her ally as she ascends the career ladder, occupying high-flying – and predominantly male – roles on the equities trading floor of Goldman Sachs and then in the CNS drug development industry. It is perhaps the four-year career break to concentrate on motherhood that triggers Kakati-Shah's deepening interest in highlighting greater understanding of diversity – which she defines as 'being invited to the party' – issues, having witnessed at first-hand the unconscious (or even conscious) bias toward mothers trying to re-enter the workforce. From this, her company was born: Uma. Uma is so-named after the Hindu goddess of strength, courage, and confidence. This suggests that the author's business (and, by implication, this book) is primarily aimed at women, but a full reading makes clear that Kakati-Shah's purpose is to advocate for any minority or marginalized group and to open the eyes of business leaders to the untapped potential at their disposal. Through Uma, she advises C-suite leaders and helps them make their organizations 'more diverse'. The content of THE GODDESS OF GO-GETTING is a deep dive into this very subject and provides a multi-faceted examination of its complexities.

"One of the strengths of this book is that a number of myths about diversity are debunked. Kakati-Shah treats the subject as the multi-layered issue that it is. As an example, she points out one of the paradoxes, explaining that some diversity practices can actually segregate and divide, rather than unite, as when policy rationale is based on '[r]everse discrimination'. She raises recognition that prejudice does not just refer to race, gender, ethnicity, etc., but encompasses the whole gamut of groups or individuals who feel 'hidden in the margins' – such as working mothers. Consequently, quota-filling is not something the writer appears to support. Rather, she seems to advocate the power of emotional intelligence and empathy in people management, which allows talent from all quarters to be acknowledged and rewarded. And while Kakati-Shah speaks of the progress being made (that so many leaders seek her guidance is testament to that), she is also realistic, reminding us that mindsets are often slow to evolve and may not keep apace with practical measures being taken. Strengthening the content of this book is the litany of supporting evidence in the form of hard evidence, quoted sources, and anecdotal detail. Even better, it is written in clear and cogent prose, making the reader's job easy.

"THE GODDESS OF GO-GETTING is a thought-provoking, useful and authentic handbook for all involved in the corporate world, covering themes that are highly topical and set to remain so for the foreseeable future."

*– Amy Hedelman, IndieReader*

# DEDICATION

To my beautiful children and leaders of tomorrow, Raahi and Reia; my darling husband Rushin, whose coparenting and unwavering support have made my endeavors possible; my dear parents Bhabani and Dinesh Kakati, who brought me into this world to make a difference; my brother Rishi, who has always supported me; and my nearest and dearest tribe of family and friends who never stopped believing in what I do. And, to the women who came before me: the mothers who helped pave the way.

# ACKNOWLEDGMENTS

There have been some truly inspirational people who have shaped my life's journey, and whose advice, mentoring, and support have made my successes possible. They taught me to embrace my experiences, challenges, and revelations with grit, resilience, and perseverance. I would like to thank:

Achyuta Samanta, Founding President of Democracy Without Borders India, Founder of Kalinga Institute of Industrial Technology (KIIT), and Kalinga Institute of Social Sciences (KISS), Member of Parliament, Lok Sabha, India
Ajay Banga, President and CEO at Mastercard
Alexandra Chapman, Senior Development Manager, US, King's College London
Andreas Bummel, Co-Founder and Director of Democracy Without Borders, and the United Nations Parliamentary Assembly Campaign
Anna Rudakova, Founder at Woman Who Matters
Aparna Kumar, Co-Chair of Global Council for the Promotion of International Trade
Ari Newsome, Trade & Investment Associate, Department for International Trade (DIT), British Consulate General, New York
Armandine Bonnard, Strategic Projects Manager, Entrepreneurship Institute, King's College London
Ashok Shah, Founder and Managing Partner, CEPS Consulting LLC

Barbara Fight, Seven-time Emmy award-winning TV Producer, and President at Organically Organized NYC

Boaz Weinstein, Founder and CIO at Saba Capital Management

Carolin Fleischmann, Professor of Digital Business and Entrepreneurship, Hochschule Ansbach, University of Applied Sciences

Catherine Claydon, Former Managing Director at Goldman Sachs

Chris Michel, Former Head of Diversity and Inclusion, Americas at Bloomberg

Clare Risman, Executive Director, St. George's Society of New York

Cristina Cuomo, Founder and Editor at Purist

David Martinelli, President of King's College London NY Alumni Committee

David Solomon, Chairman and CEO at Goldman Sachs

Ewa Urban, Director at Bank of America Merrill Lynch

Guy Saidenberg, Investor, Retired Partner at Goldman Sachs / Uma Advisor

Indra Nooyi, Former Chairman and CEO at PepsiCo

Jogen Kalita, Head of Department of Zoology, Gauhati University

Jolanta Aritz, Professor of Clinical Business Communication, Marshall School of Business, University of Southern California

Jörg Kukies, State Secretary, German Federal Ministry of Finance

Julia Gillard, Former Prime Minister of Australia and Chair of the Global Institute of Women's Leadership at King's College London

Kabir Sagoo, Former President of King's College London LA Alumni Committee

Katya Rosenblatt, Head of Business Development at Baron Capital

Maggie Arvedlund, Managing Partner at Turning Rock Partners / Uma Advisor

Marie Louise Kirk, Partner at Goldman Sachs / Uma Advisor

Marion Philadelphia, Professor of Clinical Business Communication and Academic Director of John H. Mitchell Business of Cinematic Arts Program, Marshall School of Business, University of Southern California

Mark Bordoloi, President, Global Assamese Entrepreneurship Forum

Mark Roessler, Principal, Ormiston Park Academy

Michelle Gadsden-Williams, Managing Director, Global Head of Diversity, Equity and Inclusion at Blackrock

Minna Logemann, Assistant Professor, Department of Communication Studies, Baruch College, City University of New York

Monica Berry, Principal, William Sherman PS87 Elementary School

Monique Carswell, Adjunct Professor, New York University

Munaf Ali, Global Regulatory Strategist

Octavio Avila, Student Services, Dornsife, University of Southern California

Partha Gogoi, Manager, Advanced Technologies, Accenture Federal Services

Paul Gilbert, Former CEO of MedAvante

Paul Roberts, Managing Director, PAAMCO Prisma Executive Committee

Peter Selman, Former Head of Equities at Deutsche Bank/Co-Head of Equities Trading at Goldman Sachs

Pierre Rolin, Chairman & CEO, Ankh Impact Ventures

Prabal De, Associate Professor of Economics, City University of New York

Priti Ved, Senior Security Engineer at Bloomberg

Randhir Jaiswal, Consul General, High Commission of India, New York

Rémy Luthringer, Advisor and Member of Co-Founding Investment Team at Medicxi

Rima Roy, Client Services, Turning Rock Partners / Uma Ambassador

Sabrina Pasztor, Director Culture Transformation, University of Southern California

Samuel Lalanne, Executive Director, Institutional Securities Group Global Head, Diversity and Inclusion, Morgan Stanley

Santosh Ganesh, Global Chairperson, Global Council for the Promotion of International Trade

Sebako Siame, Compliance Officer at Wells Fargo

Shahriar Zakaria, Senior Trade & Investment Manager – Americas, Department for International Trade, UK

Sridhar Chillara, Founder and Chairman, Mana TV and Mana TV International

Stanley Thangaraj, Assistant Professor of Anthropology, City College of New York

Stephen Bach, Executive Dean, King's Business School

Susan Hirshman, Private Client Advisor at Charles Schwab

Team Uma, around the world

The Alumni Team, King's College London #ForeverKings

Tonmoy Sharma, Researcher, Scientist, Author, and CEO

Usman Rabbani, Partner, Brighton Park Capital

Varun Suthra, Founding Secretary of Democracy Without Borders India, and Director of International Relations at Kalinga Institute of Social Sciences

Yanina Dubeykovskaya, Founder, Women Influence Community

Ylva Baeckstrom, Lecturer in Banking and Finance, King's Business School

# TABLE OF CONTENTS

Introduction ........................................................................1

Prologue ...........................................................................7

Chapter 1    A World of Differences: The Many Shades of
             Diversity ......................................................13

Chapter 2    Minority Complex: The Cost of Bias .........................25

Chapter 3    Why People Leave Companies: The Common
             Denominator—Inclusion, Belonging, and Decency ...36

Chapter 4    Flexibility and the Evolution of Empathy .................46

Chapter 5    Curating a Culture of Decency: Top Down ...............57

Chapter 6    Rules of the Playground: Bottom Up .......................71

Chapter 7    The Onus is on You: Accountability, Ownership, and
             Hard Work ...................................................80

Chapter 8    Unleashing Your Inner Goddess of Go-Getting: the
             Power of Confidence .......................................96

Chapter 9    Changing the Narrative ....................................110

Chapter 10   Lessons from Around the Globe............................132

Epilogue     The Tao of Uma...............................................138

Words of Inspiration............................................................141

Uma-isms ........................................................................160

Endnotes.........................................................................165

# INTRODUCTION

*"To find yourself, think for yourself."*
*– Socrates*

I was born and bred in the UK, the eldest child of Indian parents who emigrated to London from Assam in the 1970s. My father was a cardiologist and my mother a zoologist and a classically trained singer and dancer. Their customs, language, and lifestyle were the origins of my earliest lessons in life and are at the core of who I am. Though my heritage and roots are Assamese, and my childhood, adolescence, and education were very British, my upbringing was also shaped by the rich cultural traditions of the many places I lived, worked, and visited around the world.

My education eventually took me to King's College London, which served as the launching pad for my foray into the corporate world of finance. As an ambitious type-A woman, I was thrust into the consummate man's world of testosterone-driven competitiveness on the equities trading floor of Goldman Sachs in London.

It was during my time at Goldman that I first fell into diversity and inclusion work, initially by virtue of being one of only very few women on the trading floor, then as a woman of South Asian heritage. As I moved divisions, my networks grew, and I started gaining recognition both inside and outside the firm. As such, my love of giving back and empowering others was also cemented. Whether I mentored and coached colleagues at work or students and groups outside of work, there was no greater joy than seeing the fruits of your labor come together as a direct consequence of something you said, be it with someone having a spring in their step or clarity with future career direction.

Even after transitioning into global business development in the clinical trials drug development industry, my desire to empower women and girls became stronger, so I continued to mentor colleagues and friends from various parts of the world and walks of life.

I moved to New York City after I got married and now have two beautiful children, for whom I transitioned careers to raise. Even though the hours in banking or traveling across multiple time zones in the healthcare industry was tough, starting a family was the most dramatic transition I experienced. Becoming a full-time mother, I learned, also drastically expanded my skill set. Motherhood quite literally teaches skills that no corporate training program ever could. You not only become more efficient, organized, and resilient, but you also become extremely patient and an excellent negotiator and communicator. I've negotiated multi-million dollar deals with multinational corporations, but if you can negotiate with a three-year-old or a teenager, then there is no better preparation for your next interview or boardroom pitch!

When I decided to explore rejoining the professional workforce again, I had an almost four-year gap on my résumé. I was excited and eager to re-engage, so my first step back into the corporate world was a local networking event for women in New York. I donned the only professional outfit I could fit into at the time and dusted off my go-to corporate, high-heeled shoes that were certain to give me an extra boost of confidence. Even though they had been a staple of my ensemble throughout my working career, it was only a matter of minutes before I was reminded of just how painful and uncomfortable heels can be!

At the event, each attendee had to write down her name and job title on a name tag, so I wrote "SAHM" for my job. A fellow attendee greeted me, we exchanged pleasantries, and then she asked what SAHM stood for. When I explained it meant "Stay at Home Mother," she turned her back and walked away. It took a lot of courage for me to come to the event, and that single gesture was not only demoralizing as I was already low on self-esteem but solidified how so many mothers feel. Like an ignored and forgotten part of society.

When that woman walked away, I could have done one of two things. As I was standing close to the entrance, I could have gone home and cried. Believe me, I was certainly tempted to. But I was also curious. So, instead, I looked for the woman, tapped her politely on the shoulder, and asked why she reacted that way. She was taken aback, and embarrassed. Truly. She had no idea that she turned her back on me. We started chatting. It turned out that she only planned on being at the event for a short while and wanted to meet as many people from the finance industry as possible. After a while, I mentioned my background: a successful career in finance at Goldman Sachs in London that spanned a decade, followed by leading global business development in CNS clinical trials, and now on the cusp of starting my own company. In what seemed like an instant she emerged as my new best friend.

This is an example of unconscious bias, and it was one of the leading experiences I had that led me to helm Uma, which is dedicated to not only empowering women and minorities to find their voice, grow their confidence, and build leadership and resilience in the workplace, it is also focused on infusing core diversity and inclusion principles into corporate leadership and workplace culture.

There was a growing market for women and other "minorities" who were encountering obstacles in either re-entering, navigating, or progressing in the workforce, whether through the result of parental, military, family, or other duties. I also knew companies were losing existing employees due to a few reasons. First, there are corporate policies and practices that either inhibit the aforementioned circumstances or merely hired people according to a box-checking exercise. These companies perhaps had some diversity but nothing close to a truly inclusive workforce. Second, there were societal and cultural biases that placed an increased burden on women to work from home in addition to carrying out household and family responsibilities (consider the extra workload that occurred during the global pandemic of 2020).

Stemming from my own background as a British-Assamese-American, and contrary to popular belief that all Indians are the same, or all Black people are one, my own experiences from around the world allowed me to truly understand that countries and cultures are regionalized, and depending on which part of the country, state, neighborhood, or section of the country, there are different socioeconomic constructs, accents, euphemisms, fashions, diets, and values. I am reminded of that reality every day as I lead Uma workshops and talks around the world, and from the stories and experiences shared from my clients, family, and friends from the US, the UK, Latin America, and throughout Europe, Eastern Europe, Africa, the Middle East, Asia and Australia.

From my earliest days of considering a return to the professional workplace, the idea of starting my own company was there, fueled by conversations and emerging transformative trends in the marketplace. The conversations at that networking event paved the steppingstones to the future.

I named my company Uma after the Hindu Goddess who represents strength, courage, and confidence. I grew up hearing stories from my parents about this mythical goddess, Uma, a wise but evolving woman who held immense power and virtue while remaining approachable, and who relished her confidence without crossing into arrogance. Uma approached each situation and challenge with poise and grace, serving as a source of guidance and inspiration. She is a mother, daughter, sibling, and wife, and so depicts the many roles represented in our lives. Importantly, she was confident, bold, and determined, yet always maintained her composure, was kind and approachable. The more my parents would teach me about her, the more I tried to adopt those qualities that Uma embodied. She is truly a goddess of go-getting.

Today, Uma is a thriving enterprise, headquartered in New York City, with a presence in San Francisco, Los Angeles, Toronto, and London. Our focus has been working with and shaping organizational culture around the world using core diversity and inclusion principles, as well as coaching and mentoring C-suite leadership, senior managers, women, schoolgirls, veterans, and survivors of domestic violence.

Since the creation of Uma, my work has taken me around the globe advising major corporations on how to attract, retain, and develop the treasure trove of talent that surrounds us. Some of that talent already exists and is being fully leveraged within enterprises, large and small throughout the world. Some of it, however, remains hidden in the margins, waiting to be recognized and developed, waiting to innovate, waiting to produce.

So, while we see women becoming the majority of college and graduate degree students, and in leadership roles around the world, whether as a former Pakistani Prime Minister, UK Prime Minister, Australian Prime Minister, or a top tennis player in the world being African American, we must ask whether attitudes have shifted to keep pace with the actual change on the ground. The answer is clearly no.

So, when I am asked why I created the company Uma and wrote this book, *The Goddess of Go-Getting,*™ the answer is amazingly simple.

I am doing this for the millions of women and minorities before me, and I am doing this for my children. I hope to increase awareness, confidence, and in turn inspire and empower along the way. I want my son and daughter to embolden the understanding, empathy, and power of the Goddess Uma. To treat and educate others as they want to be treated themselves. To understand that every life experience is valuable. And no matter what their color, race, culture, gender, or life's situation, they should be celebrated as being unique and powerful. I want my children to hold the torch for gender equality, diversity, inclusion, and belonging going forward.

*The Goddess of Go-Getting* brings together key measurements of leadership and employee competence. For today's leaders, attributes such as empathy, listening skills, emotional intelligence, and decency are more critical than ever. As I have said so frequently in my talks around the world, to truly strive for diversity, inclusion, and equality in the workforce, these skills must be exercised like a muscle, practiced and cultivated every day, for they are crucial in managing and navigating the intricate issues of differing opinions, cultures, and emotions.

*The Goddess of Go-Getting* is a book about being successful at work, but it is not a business book. It is a book about leadership, but it is not a book about leadership. *The Goddess of Go-Getting* is a book about people and the human experience. It is about our ancestors, about us, and how we have found ourselves in this place. More specifically, it is about how we interact and co-exist in the workplace, which I refer to as The Big Four of human coexistence: Differences, Diversity, Belonging, and Decency.

*The Goddess of Go-Getting* does propose a direction, but it is not intended to be a "how to" book. Humans do not come with an instruction manual. It has never existed since the origins of the human existence, and still does not exist today. It appears we have never marked down that path. We are infinitely smarter than ever before in our history. We have learned much more about one another, but we have yet to carve the path to learn about each other's stories. It seems we're still figuring out how to coexist with one another. Apparently, the more we know about one another, our focus is we concentrate on about how different we are. It just seems we have yet to learn how much alike we are, or how to trust and respect one another. It is my hope that *The Goddess of Go-Getting* will become a part of that effort.

I invite you to join me.

Rita

# PROLOGUE

Ever since I can remember, I've been different. The way I think, how I respond, my fearlessness, and how I immerse myself in different scenarios. As a young girl, I felt out of place, but as I grew up, I realized these differences make me unique and shaped me into who I am today.

As children, you are not taught to recognize differences in gender or skin tone. Indeed, the first time I noticed I was darker than others was at school, when my friends called me names.

Did these experiences scar me? Absolutely. But they also taught me to survive, and over time, survival turned into acceptance. I developed an outer armor early on and became more resilient. I also learned to listen and be empathetic. Rather than cave into a downward spiral of name-calling, I adjusted, befriended, and educated others about who I was. There was simply no room to be a victim. I learned from a young age to adapt, fit in, and get along with others who didn't think the same way I did.

I was regarded as being different first because of my brown skin, then because I was a woman, and later as a mother looking to explore professional opportunities when I had a career gap to justify on my résumé. I know I am not alone; many others are also confronted for being a different skin color, gender, religion, and many other things.

My parents were strong, prominent members of their London-Assamese-Hindustani-Indian community. My father was one of very few Assamese doctors to make it to the UK with only two pounds in his pocket, and successfully excel as a doctor and establish himself in a foreign country, and one that wasn't particularly welcoming of Indian people. My parents had fought to get to the UK, and they thrived when so many before them had not. It was this fighting spirit that my younger brother and I had inherited early on.

They could easily have caught me each time I fell, but they had always taught me to be self-sufficient from a young age. It was this "sink or swim" messaging that guided my formative years. Giving up or playing victim was not an option. You were dealt a problem, you felt uncomfortable, then you just had to deal with it. These valuable life lessons have remained with me throughout.

Not only did I learn to be resilient and self-sufficient from a young age, but I developed the ability to see things from different—often hostile—perspectives, and when needed, seamlessly blend into my surroundings.

As a child, I found it difficult to be friends with most of the girls I knew. I had a collection of dolls from various birthday gifts, but they always remained in their boxes until a friend came to visit and would elect to play with them. I simply had no interest in playing with dolls or playing dress up. Instead, playing superheroes, computer games, or attempting to dive down an entire flight of stairs was more my thing.

My friends would therefore mostly be boys, as these were the types of activities that they seemed more interested in.

I taught myself later on how to pretend to be interested in dolls and Disney princesses, and make forced conversations that was of little interest, just so I could fit in. A skill that has actually worked well, as it has meant I can blend in easily with people from all walks of life and interests, having tried so many different things! Even as an adult, rather than receive a bouquet of flowers, bath soaps or vouchers to a spa, I would pick going on a hike, camping trip, or go-carting any day!

Whether as a young army cadet during my teenage years at school, an army scholar in the British Army after school, or stepping foot onto a male-dominated trading floor, my life's experiences taught me to fit right in, converting any initial prejudices or misconceptions due to my gender or race into respect and being judged solely by my physical, academic, or mental performance.

These life experiences are directly relevant to my current work in advising C-suite leadership and senior management in "how to be more diverse." Perhaps a reason I am asked to return is because of the real-life examples and personal anecdotes I share, with an innate ability to empathize, build trust, and convert words into action and successful outcomes.

When I was about to apply for my first job experience in my teens, my parents had a conversation with me about being different. As many fellow second-generation Indian children can no doubt relate, my brother and I had been conditioned from an early age to study harder, become smarter, and be more street savvy than anyone else in order to succeed later in life. But this time the conversation was different. My parents made the point of saying that due to being brown, I was not only competing for jobs, but had to be outstanding even to be considered for opportunities. Not just that, I was told that because I was a girl, I had to work even harder in order to be judged by my academic credentials, rather than physical appearance.

In simple terms, there are white people, and then there is everyone else. There are men, and then there is everyone else. I was part of the "everyone else" category. This conversation shaped my formative years, and led me to understanding early on what it felt like to be from a minority background and in the minority, versus in the majority or in a position of privilege—or to phrase this another way: "inferior" versus "superior." This paved the path for me to treat and educate others on differences, similarities, and how to communicate. To understand that every life experience is valuable, and no matter what color, race, culture, gender, or life situation, everyone should be celebrated as being unique and powerful.

Of the billions of us who have been characterized as "different" in one form or another, we have two choices: attempt to disguise or minimize our differences or, as I did throughout my life, embrace being different. After all, it is our differences that make us who we are.

My parents always made sure I embraced my identity. As a female with brown skin, I wasn't just a British Indian, I was a British Assamese, and only I could define who I am.

To my relief and astonishment, after that conversation I felt amazingly empowered. I felt liberated and more ready than ever to combat whatever the world awaited.

This was the conversation that shaped my formative years. It paved the path for me to receive an army scholarship to serve in the British Army as an army officer. It gave me the courage to switch degree discipline from medicine to mathematics at university. It gave me the courage to become a Pan-European sales trader on the equities trading floor of Goldman Sachs. And then to transition careers into the CNS drug development industry. And later to relocate to New York City, get married, and become a mother.

Learning to embrace and celebrate being different opened a window in my universe, which gave me an abundance of perspectives, thoughts, and ideas that became the foundation of my life and career. It was those experiences that guided me as I embarked on a career in finance, then as I negotiated deals in male-only boardrooms in the clinical trial industry, and then when I became a mother and learned how to balance the seemingly incompatible objectives of motherhood and work. And again, it was there to guide me through the launch of my company, Uma, an empowerment platform derived around diversity and inclusion principles, that advises and trains companies and senior leadership, and empowers women and minorities to gain unshakable confidence, rediscover their inner voice, and unlock their leadership potential.

The concepts of diversity, inclusion, and equality in the workplace, although immensely powerful, can also be a source of divisiveness and conflict, which creates an atmosphere of tension and bickering.

Diversity aims to "invite" people from minority backgrounds to take part, such as women and people of color. However, as a woman of color, I never want to feel like I have been given a job opportunity just because I checked both the woman and ethnic minority boxes. Rather, I want to be hired due to my credentials, professional experiences, and most importantly, my diversity of thought. Ironically, by not delving deeper and finding people who have diverse experiences, opinions, or frames of reference, we may actually be masking organizational groupthink and creating intolerance.

It wasn't until I started my career in finance that I could really apply my experiences of diversity and being different at work. As one of the very few women on the equities trading floor at Goldman Sachs in London, I initially wondered where all the women were. I wanted to ask them about their careers, see what they did day to day, and have them come and see what I do. Back then, the Women's Network did exist in London, but it had a reputation of just being women meeting for coffee, and there wasn't any professional networking or career development association with the group. I attended several of the coffee meetings, and after sharing numerous ideas and plans, we managed to change the face of the Women's Network so much that I was tasked with creating a cross-divisional footprint, which would later serve as the foundation for other European locations. In a similar vein, after congregating and joining forces with like-minded colleagues from different divisions in London, we put together a pitch to senior leadership, which later led to the successful formation of the Asian Professionals' Network.

Diversity is about bringing together different people and everyone adapting and learning from their colleagues' experiences in order to work together as a team to increase output, efficiency, and, ultimately, shareholder value. The conversations around diversity and inclusion in the workplace is a major test of leadership among CEOs and other business executives in the corporate world.

By emphasizing the importance of changing the narrative both at work and at home, we challenge the status quo of only focusing on making changes in the workplace. The onus for change is a shared responsibility by all and is harnessed over time with flexibility and commitment. Using decency as a measure of organizational leadership, and an emphasis that achieving equality doesn't mean bringing "the other" gender or race down, perhaps one day and by one person at a time, gender equality, diversity, and inclusion can be attained in our lives.

With the growing presence and economic power of women, the workplace of today is one of new attitudes, new concerns, and new expectations. And the person who leads them must have the right set of intrapersonal and interpersonal skills to do so.

Today, the premium is not on organizational management, but people management. It's about taking a talented, highly motivated, diverse workforce and blending them into high-performance teams that challenge, collaborate, and innovate. Their motivation; feeling like they belong, are valued, challenged, understood, compensated fairly, and commensurate with their worth. These are the secrets of leadership success today—and the pillars that make up *The Goddess of Go-Getting.*

# CHAPTER 1

# A World of Differences: The Many Shades of Diversity

*"Diversity... the art of thinking independently, together."*
*– Malcolm Forbes*

Growing up was an interesting experience for me. My identity was really several pieces, some complimentary, some disparate, some in conflict, and others in harmony. There was the studious and hardworking daughter of Indian immigrants pursuing a career in medicine; there was the Assamese girl at weekend family gatherings immersed in the cultural norms; there was the British girl out and about town in Western attire enjoying Latin dancing; there was the army scholar enlisted to join the British Army as an officer; and there was the strong and independent Goldman Sachs banker excited about carving her own path in the world. However, much of it was built on a foundation of a girl relentlessly teased and bullied because of her skin color and gender. Sometimes the aggressor was overt in their intent and action, other times the slights were unconscious, based on a cultural custom of deference to more "traditional" British kids at school, or a male figure at home.

Many of us share this background, growing up in two or more worlds, a foot in each but not in both, struggling to find ourselves but also struggling to find acceptance in a world that often feels like it was built for others because it *was* built by others. Many of us in one way or another still carry the burdens, battle scars, and harbor the resentments that being marginalized creates. I made a choice in my youth that despite these obstacles I would use them as fuel to forge my own path rather than be beholden to them. But just because I decided that I would not be a victim didn't mean that I would ever find these experiences to be acceptable.

Every Sunday morning my father would drive me in his weekend doctor-on-call car to my Bharata Natyam dance classes, an ancient classical temple dance form from South India. I have fond memories of meandering between traffic hotspots and dad's patient home visits, and often barely making it in time for the start of class. No matter how late we were though, or how worked up my father got from the tremendous rushing around, the dance classes were my favorite part of the week. There was no greater joy than listening to the spellbinding Carnatic music while stamping my feet rhythmically to the beat of the tabla. And yet, whether in class or at a performance, my overshadowing memory is of being the odd one out, whereas during the week, I was the dark one out. Now I was the fairest one out, with an overshadowing memory of name calling for being too light and not being invited to friends' birthday parties. Such was my dual reality and experience of color early on.

**Diversity is not monolithic**
Contrary to popular belief that all Indians are the same, or that Indians cannot be prejudiced toward other Indians, I would come to learn that throughout the world countries, and therefore cultures, are "regionalized." Depending on what part of the country, individuals come from different states and different sections of the country, and display different accents, different euphemisms, different fashions, different diets, and even different values. I am reminded of that reality every day leading Uma workshops and with my travels around the

world to and from the US, the UK, Latin America, and throughout Europe, Eastern Europe, and Asia.

In the land of my heritage India, however, that concept of regionalization has been taken to a whole different level. As Assam is tucked up in the extreme northeastern part of the country, I would see globes and world maps with Assam either left off completely or bordered off as either Burma or Bangladesh, two completely different countries. Both British Indians with heritage from other regions of India as well as first generation Indians, would flourish from stereotypical prejudices of Assamese people, including appearance, culture and traditions. This would invariably come across as harsh and hurtful. I was not only viewed differently in my motherland, the UK, but from other regions of the country of my heritage, India, too. The same is not just true for Assamese folk though. Ask any Indian whether they have received any form of prejudice from a peer, whether from a different state, "caste," or skin tone (the same with other countries sharing a border with India), and you'll get an answer in the affirmative.

In the Hulu miniseries *Mrs. America*, which is about the rise of the Equal Rights Amendment and the attempts by the anti-feminist Phyllis Schlafly to block it, Margaret Sloan-Hunter, a central, real-life character in the drama, eloquently explains to a roomful of blank faces, about tokenism in the workplace, "The phenomenon that happens where one minority is propped up to cover the entire experience of a population." She then further goes on to explain that "like the white population, we are diverse within ourselves... there is not a monolithic Black experience."

Indeed, race and diversity are not monolithic, so topics relevant in one region may be completely irrelevant in another. When deciding on hiring make up of your teams, don't just follow a checklist of demographic percentages. That may get you "equity"—as in closer to an equal split of different backgrounds—but it certainly won't be worth anything unless your team make up is reflective of the community it is serving.

## What is Diversity?

I define diversity as being invited to the party, because as a child there were so many times that I wasn't.

So, what exactly is diversity? I like to think of diversity as bringing people together of different backgrounds from different walks of life, who are representative of the communities that we live in, serve or interact with. These backgrounds are not just reflective of our places of work, but also languages and dialects spoken, dress sense, music, culinary tastes, and viewpoints.

In the modern-day work environment particularly in the US, diversity largely refers to gender, ethnicity, race, or skin color. While there are many competing rationales, the goal is generally to displace traditional power groups such as white men, in order to make room for others that are tagged as underrepresented to provide more creative and different viewpoints and solutions. While diversity as the driver of innovation is a benevolent way of thinking, the reality of how diverse individuals are selected can often cause more segregation and be divisive. After all, if you are a new hire that worked your socks off for a particular role, and all of a sudden you're known as the "diversity hire" because of your gender or skin tone, how would you feel?

## Diversity differs

As companies attempt to find an effective approach to hiring diverse individuals, the first question that senior leadership and hiring managers should be asking is, "Who am I looking to serve?" For example, the diverse population that a handloom company serving villagers in Assam, would be very different to a makeup company serving cosmopolitan citizens in Paris or New York. If the former were to hire a Black American US tax expert, one can soon see the irrelevance of that hire.

During early 2020, the Black Lives Matter movement gained momentum following the untimely death of George Floyd. For that entire month and onward, phones and email accounts were buzzing with race and diversity enquiries for companywide training sessions that would include senior leadership and grassroots employees, and across regions. However, training that may have been relevant and important to discuss with employees across the US or the UK, for example, were not necessarily relevant in a different region, such as an Indian or other Asian office. Diversity is meant to be representative of your demographic and relevant to the root issues faced in the locality.

Once the determination has been made to hire from demographics that are truly representative of the populations served, then the hiring needs to be done by equally diverse individuals, in a double-blinded clinical trial approach, so that age, gender, race, ethnicity or which golf club someone is a member at cannot impact the decision. As a result, hiring decisions are truly due to skills and qualifications of the candidates. If the talent pool is diverse to begin with, then by probability of statistics so will the employee make up.

For example, hiring more diverse talent in Russia may mean a focus on how to help Indian colleagues feel more integrated; in New York, it may mean a focus on awareness for allyship and understanding privilege; and in India, it may mean an awareness to patriarchal beliefs, treating women more equally, and extending job opportunities to those from different states and caste backgrounds.

**Don't judge a book by its cover**
The more I experienced the world both personally and professionally the more I realized there seemed to be tiered standards for different groups of people. I was never one to categorize entire blocks of people. It was much more a "take people as they come" attitude. I enjoy people in general, and like getting to know individual personalities rather than being wedded to a broad brushstroke of what someone is supposed to be inside based on how they look on the outside.

Interestingly though, I realized the world doesn't really work that way. Much of what we view as our modern society is built in large part to this mass categorization. Putting people in boxes and making assumptions which for some groups become limiting and for other more privileged groups become insulating. Oddly enough, sometimes the categorizations fit, but often they do not. The world in the last hundred years has seen an unleashing of global talent as colonialism fell and free markets rose. As countries such as India gained their independence from Great Britain or overthrew outdated and immoral systems such as apartheid in South Africa, or in the case of America, which secured a constitutional guarantee for woman's suffrage, the die for change was cast. The simultaneous rise of economic opportunity emerging from a more intertwined and peaceful world accelerated many of these movements and continue to fuel new ones. The "American Dream" became a global vision for many previously disenfranchised people and economic growth made progress for people far more attainable.

## Change takes time

While this change is a welcome development for millions, new challenges emerge as transition remains a work in progress. Although previously marginalized people are now upwardly mobile, socially forward, and economically independent, many still have mentalities that remain influenced by the old order. Underlying inequities continue, and new generations of parents and mentors struggle to explain the gap between personal progress and systemic limitations.

So while we see women become the majority of college and graduate degree students, or a large spike in Indian CEOs of tech corporations, or a Pakistani immigrant owning an American football team, or the top golfer and tennis players in the world being African American, we must ask whether attitudes have shifted to keep pace with the actual change on the ground. The answer is clearly no.

While there are many examples of progress especially at the top levels in business, culture, entertainment, etc., there remains a wide gulf between newcomers to the system and the predated attitudes they encounter. There must be a reconciliation of that gulf in order to maximize the opportunity set for the new guard but also to allow the old guard the opportunity to understand and adapt to this change.

**Think global**

The stories of those who have shaped the lives of us—our parents and their parents before them—will be superseded by stories for future generations by women and men like Rosa Parks, Mahatma Gandhi, Mother Theresa, Ruth Bader Ginsberg, Indra Nooyi, Ajay Banga, and many others. *The Goddess of Go-Getting* aspires to become one of those stories.

Since the creation of Uma, my work has taken me around the globe, advising major corporations on how to attract, retain, and develop the treasure trove of talent that surrounds us. Some of that talent already exists and is being fully leveraged within enterprises large and small throughout the world. Some of it, however, remains hidden in the margins, waiting to be recognized and developed, waiting to innovate, waiting to produce.

During a trip to Brussels, where I delivered a keynote on gender equality and inclusion at the artistic cultural center House of the Future, my eyes were immediately drawn toward a piece of "chicken"-inspired artwork by the Belgian artist and scientist Koen Vanmechelen. He notated that free-range chickens on average live to three years old. However, if they crossbreed across cultures they live until eight to ten years old. If the examples of chickens is anything to go by, then diversity is a good thing and even leads to longevity!

A diverse workforce increases representation of more people with diverse experiences, creating a pool of talent with different points of view, and this is incredibly useful to facilitating open-mindedness and problem solving.

**Take heed of the data**

Despite calls for change, however, gender diversity in top leadership at US companies has barely budged. As of 2018, research shows that only five percent of CEOs at large, publicly traded companies were women,[1] and according to data by Equilar, the ratio of women on executive boards of the largest publicly traded companies in the US is only one in five.

According to a research report by Morgan Stanley,[2] investing in gender diversity at the workplace is not only profitable for both companies and investors but that more gender-diverse companies offer slightly better returns with lower volatility. More gender diversity, particularly in corporate settings, can translate to increased productivity, greater innovation, better decision-making, and higher employee retention and satisfaction. "In essence, companies that screen better for gender diversity metrics are higher quality companies using... [Morgan Stanley's]... other standard financial metrics," says Chief US equity strategist Adam Parker on the Global Quantitative report, "Putting Gender Diversity to Work: Better Fundamentals, Less Volatility."

In addition, ninety-one percent of workers employed at organizations with formal diversity and inclusion initiatives such as Udemy[3] think the impact on the workplace is significant. Interestingly, sixty-three percent of men think their companies are doing a pretty good job supporting diversity, compared to only twenty-three percent of women saying there is more room for improvement, according to Lean In (leanin.org).[4]

**Doing diversity right: unite, don't divide**

The concepts of diversity, inclusiveness, and equality in the workplace are immensely powerful forces, but can also be a source of divisiveness and conflict creating an atmosphere of tension and bickering. On the bright side, CEOs, managers, and employees can overcome these forces through proper awareness, training, and of course practice. I like to equate a company working toward diversity and inclusion to a type of muscle memory, which like any other habit, needs constant practice and regular, actionable feedback. After all, diversity and inclusivity are more than buzzwords or business goals but values that must be understood, internalized, and subsequently deployed correctly in order to avoid an unexpected backlash of reverse discrimination.

So when companies hire me to "make them diverse," or request that I help them structure a "Black" or "South Asian" affinity group, for example, my first reaction is to understand the rationale behind such a move before moving on to educate the leadership in the strategic manifestations of creating a diverse workforce. After all, there is a subtle, but fine line between curating a meaningful path to achieving a firm's diversity goals, versus creating reverse discrimination which ends up alienating team members instead.

An example is a Los Angeles–based client of mine in the film industry. They called me in to "fix" their issues of attrition of mostly women, but also people of color. It so turned out that they had invested a majority of their diversity budget into creating affinity groups for women and people of color. There would be luxurious spa days for the women once a month and cultural cuisines and musical celebrations for the employees of color. However, the men—white men to be precise—were now feeling left out. Why could they not go on a spa day? Why were they not invited to enjoy some of the multinational cuisines? Long story short, they felt reverse discrimination, they complained, the affinity groups were cancelled, employees started to leave, and so Uma was promptly called in to fix the issue. And fix it we did. We conducted a company-wide roleplaying exercise to showcase the meaning of being in the minority, feeling inferior, and how to address these issues with allyship, understanding privilege, decency, empathy, and kindness.

Diversity aims to "invite" people from different backgrounds, such as women, members of the LGBTQIA+ community, military veterans, a particular culture, those who are neurodiverse, and people from a particular racial grouping.

However, as a woman and one of color, I never want to feel like I've been given a job opportunity just because I have checked both the woman and minority boxes. Rather, I would like to be hired due to my credentials, professional experiences, and most importantly, my diversity of thought. However, time and time again, most organizations who have apprised diversity as a goal do so superficially for a diversity box-checking exercise.

## Diversity of thought

Oddly enough, by not delving deeper and finding people who have different experiences and different opinions or frames of reference, we may be masking organizational groupthink and creating intolerance of different opinions and worldviews. Does it matter if you have men and women of different racial and ethnic groups who all think the same? Or is it better to have an environment that cherishes diversity of thought that can allow for more rounded and relevant views. Is an organization better off with this construct, or does a lack of diverse views and opinions actually create a competitive disadvantage?

The concept of diversity and what constitutes a "diverse workforce" has changed dramatically since the early 1990s, not only in scope, but in complexity as well. At the turn of the century, our predecessors were confronted with only one realistic challenge: the issue of equality between men and women. Today, as the changes have mirrored those in society, the concept has mushroomed to become a complex web of issues that have collectively been referred to as the intermingled topics of diversity and inclusion. As largely as a mirror into those of society, the conversation of diversity and inclusiveness in the workplace has become a major test of leadership among CEOs and other business executives in the corporate world, and a major topic of debate and analysis in the world of social and behavioral scientists.

## Differences drive diversity

But to those of us who are directly affected by the topic, its definition and parameters are much more to the point, captured by one simple word, and that is being regarded as "different."

Some of our differences are a function of birth, while others are assumed by circumstance. In either situation, societies inflict its views in the same way, as is the anguish and repercussions of its recipients, be they from birth or circumstance. As did I, so many individuals confront not just one aspect of being different, but one, two, three, and more. I was regarded as being different firstly as being of brown skin, a woman, and later a working mother with a "gap" to fill on my résumé. Others confront being a different skin color, gender, religion, and many other aspects of their multiple differences.

## Be accountable

So how do you hold C-suite or senior leadership accountable for their firm's diversity goals? You could start by linking CEO pay to these diversity goals. As the conversation around racial equality and diversity gains momentum in the corporate world, some business leaders say that tying annual bonuses to those efforts may accelerate companies' hiring goals. According to recent data from 2020 cited by the *New York Times*, only seventy-eight of approximately three thousand companies surveyed say a portion of their CEOs pay was linked to accomplishing diversity objectives. Tying those to compensation and releasing clear targets would also hold companies more accountable, say some hiring experts.

As a company increasingly thinking about structuring diversity and inclusion initiatives as part of a broader firmwide taskforce, here are some key steps to get you started:

- Understand the diversity makeup of the local communities served by your regional office
- Compare this demographic with the existing makeup of your organization
- Speak to a cross section of employees across level of seniority and across the organization to understand where discrimination and bias actually exists
- Engage and listen to any minority groups to understand their lived experiences
- Examine whether your policies and processes are truly inclusive

- Look at how and from where you currently attract and recruit new talent

- Build a roadmap and set clear targets for diversity and inclusion

- Hold senior managers and teams accountable, by building in key deliverables to their annual reviews

The single most effective and powerful thing that we can do right now to improve leadership teams is to add diversity. After all, diverse teams are known to excel at problem solving and understanding customers' wants and employees' needs. The result is that such teams will make better decisions, drive more innovation, and ultimately create more opportunities for growth.

In today's world, diverse thinking within your leadership teams is the key ingredient to business success. So the next time you are faced as a senior leader with a saturated board room, rather than walk away pull up another chair to the table and invite a diverse colleague to sit there. Then do what you need to do in order to amend your bylaws, rules, and traditional values.

Of the billions of us who have been characterized as different in one form or another, we have two choices: to attempt to disguise or minimize our differences, or as I did throughout my life, embrace being different, for as goddess Uma would have guided, it is our differences that make us who we are.

# CHAPTER 2

## Minority Complex: The Cost of Bias

*"[P]eople usually see what they're already looking for . . ."*
*– Veronica Roth, Allegiant*

Not so long ago, I was an executive in the world of clinical trials leading business development globally within the central nervous system drug development industry. I was on first name terms with key opinion leaders and C-suite leadership at the world's leading pharmaceutical and biotechnology companies. I traveled around the world, attending upmarket conferences and fancy invitation-only dinners with the movers and shakers of the pharma world. I had a good life and loved my job.

In between my travels and packed work schedule, I got married and five wedding ceremonies later, moved from London to New York City. I loved the Big Apple—the cosmopolitan city that never sleeps, and so couldn't wait to move. However, after I arrived, a different reality awaited me.

I took a yellow taxicab from JFK to my new apartment, paid the driver, and when he returned my credit card, I heard him utter something under his breath and comment, "Learn to speak English." "I am English!" I thought to myself, but regardless, that was the first experience in my new city, and I felt like an outsider. My initial excitement dissipated and for a moment I felt like I didn't belong. I was now in the minority with my strong English accent and for that, I felt inferior.

It is important to clarify that when I say minority. I don't just mean ethnic minority, but am including whoever happens to be in "the minority" within the environment they are in. This has included, but not limited to mothers, military veterans, girls and women in STEM, members of the LGBTQIA+ community, survivors of domestic violence, and anyone who has relocated. Simply put, if you are in the minority in a roomful of people and have a feeling of inferiority because of it, you are deemed a minority. As an example, if you're the only light- or dark-skinned person in the room, the only woman in a boardroom, or man in a parent association meeting, and are made to feel conscious about it, then you are a minority. Put another way, if you feel as though you're the poster child for your culture or background, then that includes you. The reverse also rings true. For example, if you're one of the masses, or majority, then you are in a position of privilege, or power.

Bias is something we all have, and research shows it takes only seven seconds5 to formulate a first-time opinion about someone. Is this what happened to the taxi driver, I wonder? Did he merely make the comment about my grasp of the English language based upon the image of me with my suitcase, being picked up from the airport and my skin tone? Perhaps he didn't even hear my voice clearly enough to notice my accent but reacted in haste in response to a long working day.

"Bias" is a rather harmless word. In effect, it is how we are brought up—our cultural, societal, and environmental surroundings—which formulate ideas, views, and ultimately our belief system. It can be as innocent as speculating on the weather or choosing an item from a restaurant menu because it reminds you of a childhood memory. It could be based on one's perception of educated information, others' opinions, or even the proverbial "old wives' tale." Whichever way it is formulated, the word itself is innocuous.

Biases can be overtly conceived, or they can be mindless, almost unconscious such that sometimes we are aware of these, and other times our views or beliefs are so mechanical that we do not even notice them. Or as R.D. Laing once said, "If I don't know but don't know that I don't know, I think I know."

Unconscious biases, also referred to as implicit biases, are the underlying attitudes and stereotypes that we unconsciously attribute to another person or group of people, which in turn, affect how we interact with them, and make decisions about them. We all have them, and knowingly or unknowingly, we bring them with us into the workplace.

They can be ingrained in us by a synthesis of fables and opinions embedded into our culture, and therefore, into our belief set. Beliefs such as "The best time to prepare your garden is after Easter Sunday," or "Do not go out in the sun for fear of becoming dark," which may seem quite innocent if you are accustomed to hearing it, but inadvertently conveys the message that "fair is superior" and "dark is inferior."

Although biases can be generally benign, serving as a source of guidance and instruction for individuals and cultures, they can also become sinister. When biases have detrimental or harmful impact on others, the word is no longer benign and instead becomes entwined with other words such as prejudice, discrimination, or bigotry.

That is when the word takes on a completely different, more ominous connotation, becoming associated with various ills of our societies and cultures. That is the word rising beyond the level of innocent and preconceived beliefs to actions that adversely affect the lives of others.

Bias also affects our perspective; a singular lens to our own feelings based generally upon our own experiences and value system that we were brought up with.

An example of perspective leading to prejudice is your reaction to the question, "Where are you from?" As I came to realize over the years of living in the States, born-and-bred Americans quite often take offense from this question and respond no matter how pushed they are about their heritage with the name of the town they were born in. Naturalized Americans or Europeans/Asians, on the other hand, appear to welcome the question, and in fact get offended if not asked. Personally, I love being asked where I am from so that I can delve into my British upbringing and Assamese heritage. It's the questions and conversation that follows that drive me, rather than the thought that someone is questioning my right to be there.

It is bias and our perceptions that ultimately manifest as prejudice, prejudices that not only affect job opportunities and who to become friends with, but also in a patriarchal sense. This is ingrained in certain societies and cultures such as those in Southeast Asia. And it is these beliefs and value systems that then spread across the world as families emigrate and relocate, taking along their cultures and beliefs with them too.

Patriarchal and cultural biases are of extraordinary relevance, for they shape the viewpoints stemming from value systems that come from your upbringing, in terms of what is deemed culturally and gender appropriate, or not. For example, a certain set of rules for the way a girl is "expected" to dress or sit, or which gender should pay the bill for dinner at the end of a first date.

When we think of "Western countries," such as the US, Canada, and the UK, they are made up of so many different cultures, which come with their own belief systems and biases, stemming from their own societies. As a result, one culture may appear prejudiced toward another culture or religion. For example, I am of Indian heritage, but while growing up I have been privy to countless family and community gatherings. It was quite usual to hear uncles and aunties (meaning friends of parents rather by relation) talk down upon about another culture. Another example is that with other Indian friends it was quite common to hear derogatory remarks made about people from Assam. Appearance, facial features, skin tone, you name it. As the years went by and as I experienced different cultures, I noticed this was quite common. For example, between the different indigenous tribes around Lago Atitlan in Guatemala, or between the northeastern Bahians and southern people of Brazil, or Cantonese speaking Chinese in Hong Kong, and Mandarin speaking Chinese across parts of mainland China. The list goes on.

Complex as it all is, within all these cultures and microcultures, societies and micro-societies, there has always been a favorable bias toward fairer, taller and "fitter"-looking people, which extends next to women within those same benchmarks, and then anyone else (read those within the LGBTQIA+ or physically handicapped communities) cast into second-class citizenry.

As a woman of color, I can safely say that we have been fighting this battle for years and have only recently begun to climb out of this pigeonhole, despite being instrumental in so many of the innovations we enjoy today.

In Asian societies, it is often common for women to question their worth. From childhood your culture dictates a certain type of behavior and etiquette that basically puts your needs at the bottom of everyone else's. This could be anything from being the one expected to serve guests, eat last, cook and clean, and not be allowed to leave the house to meet friends, whereas there are a completely different set of rules for your male friends or brothers. This can lead you to question your self-worth, and overtime ignore your potential.

It was Ada Lovelace who worked with Charles Babbage in 1842 to develop what is now the computer.[6] Dr. Shirley Jackson was the first black woman to receive a PhD from MIT in 1973,[7] and while working at Bell Laboratories, conducted research that led to many other innovations, such as the portable fax machine, touchtone telephone, solar cells, and fiber optic cables. Then there's the Black American mathematician Katherine Johnson,[8] whose calculations of orbital mechanics at NASA were critical to US spaceflights. Lastly, there's and the English chemist and fellow King's College London alumna, Rosalind Franklin,[9] whose work was crucial in discovering the structure of DNA.

Fortunately, in the West at least, there have been more prominent strides taken to tackling such biases, but as with any other diversity and inclusion effort, there is still much work to be done. Take for example, socioeconomic status and the perception of one's job, for which robust training, education, and leading by example is needed in tackling unconscious bias.

Our education, our practices, and our governmental policies have advanced to become more inclusive and more accommodating. Realizing that some countries and some governments have advanced further than others, in general we are a more welcoming society, recognizing class and individual differences, from race, gender, physical limitations, and sexual orientation.

Contrary to archaic beliefs inherited by past generations, darker-skinned races and women have proven to equal, if not surpass, men and lighter-skinned generations across scientific, educational, and industrial endeavors. It's these contributions that establish the "erosion" of biases.

To evolve is to continue, to advance, to improve. And in the domain of inclusivity and openness, there is still work to be done. And there is more untapped value to be discovered.

The definition of "diversity" is expanding at an unprecedented rate. We have incorporated segments of our society that were once safely cordoned off, thought to be of little value to the mainstream of progress.

Yet, within this evolution (or revolution as some may call it), there is a segment of our society that stands as the ultimate paradox of inclusivity. They are the bedrock of our society, the very reason for our existence, yet whose value is debated, questioned and dismissed by many, even today.

That is the working mother.

Regardless of whether our mothers worked at an office in an external career or in the home in an internal career such as being a domestic engineer or caregiver, she was always working. The value and contribution of our mothers is unquestioned. They are bright, resourceful, of endless energy, and the archetypes of getting multiple tasks done simultaneously. Personally, I recall my mother cleaning the house, preparing meals, and helping my brother and I with our homework, seemingly all at once.

By almost every measure, we would place our mothers on par, if not above our fathers. Yet when the word "working" is placed in front of the word "mother," attitudes seem to shift, even for those who proved their value in the workplace before they transitioned into careers of raising their families.

Yet the biases persist, with managers, CEOs, and even with human resource professionals. Bit by bit, however, we're chipping away. More and more, companies are recognizing the incremental value working mothers bring to their organizations. But there still too many are missing out on that value. Perhaps, the fear is that somehow embracing the very essence of womanhood and motherhood may diminish their value as an employee. Or that once they become a mother, they will have conflicting priorities, unable to balance their responsibilities as a mother with their responsibilities at work.

Perhaps theirs is a holdover bias from a previous generation. But the evidence is the exact opposite. In study after study, research and business leaders have demonstrated that working mothers, especially upon their return to the workplace, not only equal their male and non-mother female counterparts in areas like reliability, productivity, and innovation, but surpass them. The study conducted by the Federal Reserve Bank of St. Louis,10 revealed that over the course of a 30-year career, mothers outperformed women without children at almost every stage of the game, and that mothers with at least two children were the most productive of all.

However, employers don't often see this. Questions such as balancing work and life priorities or keeping up with the latest advances in technology and corporate policies are often front of mind. Though illegal to ask in many places like the US, the real, unspoken question is, "Can you truly be relied upon to compete, produce, and innovate at the same levels now that you're a mother?"

I encountered these same questions, both spoken and unspoken. After transitioning careers, relocating to the US, and transitioning careers to raise my two children, new biases emerged. Even though the four years raising my family was by far the most challenging and hardest job I had ever done, with plenty of professionally transferable skills such as communications, project management, working in constantly changing environments, leadership and negotiations, prospective employers did not see it this way. In the eyes of employers, I was no longer ambitious and the proverbial "gap" on my résumé translated to not being career focused and a quitter.

The truth is, that when I was ready to re-explore the workforce, my preparedness in terms of technological advances, financial jargon, and knowledge wasn't as relevant to the interviewer as the perception I gave. In the end, it boiled down to the hiring manager's own biases and the level of confidence I exuded.

The impact of perception is far greater than can be imagined, and there will always be some level of divide between different viewpoints. What we can do, however, is be aware of these and do our part to be more mindful to not place judgment because of it.

For example, as someone who has been both a working and stay-at-home mother, I have heard several comments over the years of working mothers often perceiving stay-at-home mothers as lazy or not doing anything all day. On the flip side, working mothers have been deemed neglectful of their children and families. Same is true for breastfeeding versus bottle feeding babies, and so on. This is clearly not gender related but perception related. When you are in one "group" you bond with them, and then ensues a subconscious "them" versus "us" scenario.

To understand perception even better, think of being a passenger in an Uber, taxi, or car in a busy metropolis like New York City, and trying to make a light before it turns red. If you are in the car, you may well wish pedestrians would "get out of the way" to let you make the light. Similarly, if you now get out of the car and try to rush across the road to make the walk sign, you may well think "Hey, you almost ran me over." So perceptions are really subjective and can change in a moment. When you are on one side, you tend to bond and empathize with that side, and when on the other, the reverse is true.

Another example is fathers being treated differently at preschool drop off. In this case they are in the minority, with mothers and caregivers usually being more common. I used to see and hear of times when fathers would be close to being idolized for dropping off or picking up a preschooler, whereas a single mother fitting in pickups during shift-change jobs would receive yet another verbal warning for being two minutes late.

On the reverse, we know that statistically, eighty percent of startups fail, and that there are generally more men-led startups in Silicon Valley compared to women. This makes it more common for the partners or spouses to be the breadwinners, and the startup parent—usually the father—is seen at school drop offs and pick-ups more commonly, and so by extension of that, more of my coaching and mentoring clientele in the Bay Area of the West Coast are therefore men. They almost unanimously reported feelings of feeling left out, singled out and even being "sneered" at by fellow parents, more often mothers in school parents' association meetings, hearing comments such as, "I can't believe they don't have a real job."

So being a minority is indeed complex, and because there are so many facets to it many organizations appear to glaze over them. On the contrary, I made it my life's mission through Uma to change, or call out, these biases and perceptions, and by doing so, create awareness that could then build empowerment and unshakable confidence. I wished to educate businesses, corporations, and society around the world of the intrinsic value they are missing by being blind to this extraordinary segment of our society, and simultaneously empower those seeking to rejoin their careers, or progress in an existing one, with the tools of confidence, leadership, and resilience.

The Women in the Workplace 2020 report from LeanIn.org, in partnership with McKinsey,[11] highlights that women, especially women of color, are twenty-five percent more likely to have been laid off or furloughed during the global COVID-19 pandemic crisis and that "working" mothers are experiencing burnout for having to always work a "double shift," namely a full day of work, combined with homeschooling, caring for children, doing household labor, and all without any support system such as school, childcare, or family support. So if anything, there needs to be a shift in mindset, resources, and shared responsibilities to even out the playing field.

The motherhood penalty is an example that demonstrates that women with children face a wage penalty of around ten percent to fifteen percent compared with those without. Another study, published in the *American Journal of Sociology*, showed that when people have to decide about hiring fictitious candidates, they discriminate heavily against women perceived to be parents. They think they deserve seven percent less in their starting salaries and should get fewer promotions in the future. According to the authors, mothers were judged as significantly less competent and committed than women without children and were also held to harsher performance and punctuality standards. Mothers were allowed significantly fewer times of being late to work, and they needed a significantly higher score on the management exam than non-mothers before being considered hirable.

Another example is a study by *Harvard Business Review*[12] that found if you cited a career "gap" on your résumé and the reason for that gap was motherhood, you are fifty percent less likely to be called for a job interview, than if the reason for the gap was due to redundancy. Put another way, you are better off getting fired than being a mother, such is the stigma and very real bias against mothers.

Not only is this an incredible loss of talent to the workforce, but research shows it costs companies between 1.5 and three times a departing worker's salary to hire and train a new employee,[13] [14] so companies are suffering a significant dent to their bottom line. If you look at the Bureau of Labor and Statistics' monthly data, this extra cost to the US economy overall is in excess of twenty billion dollars.[15]

The cost of bias isn't just financial though. By allowing someone to "feel" like the odd one out, and that they are in the minority, or inferior, means you are questioning their identity and have indirectly cost them their confidence.

There is an onus on everyone, from C-suite leadership in corporations, to grassroots employees spanning across industries, to the school system across academia, to bring awareness of unconscious bias in order to address it.

Awareness of minorities as a major pool of talent is the first step in creating a tapestry of a workplace culture that turns a clear eye toward opportunities for all its workers, and, as a result, attracts, retains, and develops their talent in a way that improves its metrics across the board.

Companies are adjusting themselves to prevent unconscious bias with the use of artificial intelligence algorithms, to blind, or strip résumés of any salary information and promotion details. In other words, stripping out any identifying "minority" triggers such as race, gender, or age.

Overall, being aware of your own value system, and educating yourself to learn and understand about others' differences is the key to broadening mindsets and welcoming colleagues to the team that are not just like you, whether it is experience, sports affiliation, educational background, ethnicity, or gender.

# CHAPTER 3

## Why People Leave Companies: The Common Denominator—Inclusion, Belonging, and Decency

*"Their goal wasn't to stand out because of their differences;*
*it was to fit in because of their talents."*
*– Margot Lee Shetterly, Hidden Figures*

After I moved to the US, I immersed myself in my work, continuing to travel around the world, this time returning to New York City as my base rather than London.

The next day after I arrived, I applied for a local American Express credit card, as my current Amex was registered to my UK address. It was rejected. Something about not having any credit history. I felt like an outsider yet again. I hadn't realized the reality of having to build "local" credit history from scratch, especially as by that time I had built up over a decade's worth of UK credit. As a strong and independent, type-A personality woman, this rocked my boat a little. The reality had hit me, that I had gone from being financially independent to now being financially dependent. I had to be my husband's "plus 1" rather than peer, at least for the first few months, until I could reestablish myself. It was like my identity was under question and I felt irrelevant—again, inferior—and called out yet again for being "foreign." I felt as if I didn't belong and consequently became increasingly resistant to wanting to absorb my new country. I still remember moving to the US around the time of the Royal Wedding (of William and Kate) and becoming overly patriotic. Whereas if I had been in the UK, I perhaps would have watched the wedding on the television (though as a "background" watcher, slipping in and out of key moments). However, now I had to be at the one British pub nuzzled under Brooklyn Bridge at 4 A.M. New York time, to watch every detail of the ceremony!

I spent the days immersing myself in my work. If I ever heard an English accent in the background somewhere, anywhere, I would immediately gravitate toward the conversation and strike up a conversation with a random stranger. Such was my longing to feel at home.

During my CNS drug development days, I was pregnant with my son, and remember battling through morning sickness (which should really be called day-long sickness!) on flights and client meetings. I would tip the bartender on the side to pour me water with a slice of lime, each time I or a colleague ordered a gin and tonic for me— my go-to post-dinner drink! If for no other reason, the business development circuit was fierce, and you were judged by your ability to interact with and "keep up" with clients. I was of course well versed and very comfortable with blending in and keeping up, so to speak, especially because of my previous decade spent in finance. This was something different though. I was pregnant, and I didn't want anyone knowing about it. I was feeling nauseated most of the time, and any distraction—denial, if you like—actually helped distract me from the frequent restroom visits.

As my pregnancy progressed, and I started to go beyond the awkward "maybe she has just put on some extra pounds" glances, I sat down with my boss to discuss the plan for my clients' accounts and coverage during the time of giving birth. I hadn't planned on taking any time off at this stage, as this was more informational, but I was, however, aware in the back of my mind that had I been in the UK I would have received up to a year of maternity leave, with some mentoring when returning to work. However, when I discussed this with my boss, he offered up six weeks leave (not months, but weeks), which I would have to file for as "disability leave." I was beyond shocked. I was about to produce a new life, and this conversation was supposed to be joyful and full of hope. But instead, I felt reduced from being at the very top of my global business development game, to nothing. In an instant, I felt like an outsider in the business I helped to build.

I quit my job and spent the next four years immersed into the joys of fulltime motherhood, which was by far the most challenging and hardest job I had ever done. Not only are you on call twenty-four hours, seven days a week, but you are constantly sleep-deprived, can never take a sick day, and are having to balance multiple schedules and household activities, all the time. Not only that, you become a communications expert, and a fierce negotiator! After all, as I frequently share in my talks, if you can you negotiate with a toddler or teenager, there is no one on this planet that you cannot take on!

I often think back to that conversation with my boss and to what would have made me stay at the job. If only the tone and language used was different, or if only he had started by saying, "Congratulations," or offered up some internal resources to help navigate this lifechanging journey or introduced me to other senior women in the industry who had taken their maternity leave and successfully returned to their previous roles. Everything would have been different. If only I had felt valued and respected. If only.

My story is merely a drop in the ocean of the hundreds of thousands of women and minorities within the workforce that are not seen or heard. So many women have left and are continuing to leave the workforce. They are marginalized and eventually leave. Whether they are veterans, women in STEM or finance, spouses of those who have relocated, single mothers, or those that balance homeschooling or household duties, members of the LGBTQIA+ community, or any other minority group, they are continuing to leave the workforce or unable to return, due to inadequate support, resources and leadership.

It's a common fallacy that people don't leave bad companies, they leave bad bosses. In my case, this wasn't solely the fault of my boss. It was a combination of the system, the lack of training, empathy, and truth be told, lack of compassion and understanding from the entire leadership team.

In fact, a *Harvard Business Review* study[16] with Facebook shows that people leave jobs that are unfulfilling (not necessarily underpaid). A quote from the study suggests that "Most companies design jobs and then slot people into them. Our best managers sometimes do the opposite: When they find talented people, they're open to creating jobs around them."

For most businesses, labor costs are its number one expenditure and in many cases account for more than seventy percent of its total costs. Yet, according to a survey by the HR consulting firm, Paycor,[17] employers spend less than fifteen percent of their time and effort managing this most significant cost item. From recruiting to compensation, to training and managing its workforce, employers typically delegate those activities to its human resources department, with varying degrees of oversight and guidance.

As in my case, when employees become disenchanted or disengaged, and then leave as a consequence, these costs are driven even higher due to the added recruiting time, effort, extra compensation, training, and development required in the interim.

As we have seen, hiring the right employee is only half the battle. The other half is about retaining that employee and creating positive work conditions to not only improve their productivity, but their overall enjoyment and likeliness to stay. The indirect costs of employee attrition are anywhere from 1.5 to three times greater than if they were to stay.[18] Not just the costs to replace them, but their acquired knowledge, general knowhow of the company culture, plus of course, extra workload created for remaining team members until a replacement is hired. In fact, research on companies in the United States equated this cost to nearly $1.5 million per manager.

It would seem that for that kind of investment companies would want to treat carefully.

Ultimately, if you don't feel respected, valued, or heard, you are more likely to leave your job. After all, no one wants to feel ignored or irrelevant. In my case, a combination of not feeling included, feeling as I was the only one, and feeling like I didn't belong, with a manager that didn't understand how to navigate my situation, snowballed into my decision to leave.

## Belonging

A sense that one belongs is a fundamental human need and a feeling that is far more powerful than any diversity and inclusion strategy. It's a feeling that we all crave, and transcends cultures, countries, and languages. In this chapter, we delve into the reasons people leave companies, and identify the common denominator of inclusion, belonging, and decency.

In our journey of diversity, inclusion, and belonging, one way of thinking about this is that if diversity can be equated to being offered a seat at the boardroom table, inclusion is actually being reserved a spot and having a chair pulled out for you to sit in, and belonging is where you feel comfortable enough to speak up and have your voice be heard.

Companies collate data from exit interviews, and with the power of hindsight realize there could have been ways of either predicting the run-up to events or preventing the employee from leaving, before they are sitting in front of HR. Looking at the situation with fresh eyes and increased awareness is one option. To benefit from retained (rather than re-trained) talent, companies must open their eyes: see and really hear why people are leaving, and then look to thoughtfully incorporate solutions to address the issues. This not only keeps companies accountable by living their core values, it also measures their success.

A company came to us when they lost women who left the workforce after having children, and they were struggling to bring women returners back in. Our first task was to analyze why they wanted to specifically target this group of diverse talent. When companies think of diverse talent, there is often a checklist of pre-empted experiences or values that come to light. However, if HR teams set out instead to be inclusive, meaning going beyond an applicant's résumé and taking the time to understand the whole person, thereby looking for reasons to *include* rather than *exclude* their application, then things could be quite different. And indeed they were. We completely overhauled their hiring practices and worked to formulate new hiring criteria that included training existing senior leadership and management, holding them accountable at year-end reviews with quarterly employee check-ins and surveys, structuring an inclusive return-to-work program, and putting in place robust buddy, mentoring, and sponsorship goals. A turnaround is an understatement of the significant impact our work made.

Companies that are successful at attracting, retaining, and developing talent have another common denominator in addition to culture: they walk the talk. They are not only aware of the connection between flexibility, inclusiveness, diversity, and empathy to employee well-being and corporate success, they keep themselves and their employees active and accountable to maintaining a culture that empowers people to maintain and practice those values daily.

Ultimately, company culture is the missing puzzle piece as to whether employees leave a company or stay. According to Deloitte,[19] nearly twenty percent of twenty-four- to thirty-five year-olds reported a company's reputation for ethical behavior, diversity, and inclusion as well as workplace wellbeing were important factors when choosing where to work. Similarly, according to Staples,[20] sixty-three percent of employees wouldn't accept a job without first knowing that the organization is actively inclusive of women, minorities, and people with disabilities. There are other well-known reasons specific groups of individuals leave companies, ranging from parental leave, salary, sexual harassment, and of course, poor managers. According to a survey by The Balance Careers,[21] other reasons of workplace discrimination include age, religion, country or region of origin.

## Inclusion

On a trip to Russia where I was to present at the Woman Who Matters Forum in Moscow, I was going as an ambassador of the Western world, an influencer, and thought leader in diversity and inclusion, who had the specific task of empowering Russian companies and the women attending, with noteworthy dialogue and the tools to change cultural stereotypes.

To prepare for my talks, I researched past Russian speakers and how they conveyed information. I didn't want to just read off slides or lecture the attendees. I needed to make an impact. My mission after all was to impact and inspire companies in Russia and the women attending, so I had to achieve what I had traveled so far to do.

My opening talk was a keynote on diversity and inclusion. I didn't present any slides but chose instead to have a personal conversation with the audience, which was a very different approach to historical Russian speeches. I wanted to have a simple chat, so I spoke slower than usual, with an effort to really break down concepts that, particularly in the West, we take for granted such as the difference between diversity and the separate but hand-in-hand concept of inclusion.

The keynote opened by inviting a show of hands to the three-thousand-strong audience of Eastern European and Russian leadership, senior management and thought leaders, by asking whose workplaces actively practiced diversity and inclusion. Pretty much a sea of hands, about two thirds of the attendees, went up. One attendee volunteered that as Russia and India share a friendly relationship, they regularly hire Indians to work in Russia. On the back of that, I asked the audience for another show of hands, this time anyone who had heard of the Indian festival Diwali. Most hands were raised. I congratulated the room on being "diverse." Next, I asked for a further show of hands, this time for whomever *celebrated* Diwali with their Indian colleagues. I counted fewer than ten hands, which at 0.3% of a roomful of three thousand people, was a very telling story. This was an example of diversity without inclusion.

There cannot be true diversity without an understanding and practice of inclusivity.

During the few days I was in Russia, I was given a private interpreter. For my final talk, I was faced with quite a bit of resistance to have my interpreter sit on stage as I spoke. Despite resistance, I fought for my interpreter, Alyona Cherkashina, to not only be permitted on stage, but to sit center stage, right next to me while I was giving my talk. She had been shadowing me the whole time I was in Russia, and if it weren't for her, I wouldn't have had the impact I had during my other speeches. Not only that, this was also real life, a real-time example of inclusion, which was the topic of my speech. We went over a few key conclusions to ensure they were translated in the intended context. We worked hand in hand. I spoke, paused, and then she spoke. Same pace, same eye contact, same emphasis on key words. It worked! The audience reacted. There were multiple comments on the power of our words and how they meant something. With that, I can say I achieved what I had traveled so far to do.

I had a great time exploring not only the beauty of Russia but being part of an extraordinary development in empowering its women.

When tackling employee retention companies ought to take a wholistic approach and look at their overall corporate strategy. Building confidence and empowering returning employees is a start, but what is paramount is the need to make a concerted effort stemming from senior management, to increase inclusivity rather than focus solely on hiring diverse candidates.

Since the emergence of the corporate culture, theories have abounded about what caused people to leave their company. There is the "job embeddedness theory," which suggests that people stay in their jobs because they become invested in their connections to co-workers, the company, and the community. If they leave their company, the theory suggests, the employee could be sacrificing those linkages that have become a critical element of their social fabric.

Then there is the theory associated with Maslow's hierarchy of needs,[22] suggesting that the basic needs of job security and a reliable paycheck could supersede the matters of job satisfaction or their relationships with co-workers or bosses.

Or there is Herzberg's motivator/hygiene theory.[23] Herzberg says that those two major factors, the motivators and the hygiene elements, determine whether employees choose to stay with their companies. The "motivator" factors, according to the theory, include recognition, achievement, work, growth, and advancement; and the "hygiene" factors include a relationship with boss, supervision, salary, relationship with colleagues, work conditions, and the company's policy.

Then, there are the matters of simple economics, and family situations, which were believed by many theorists to be the primary determinants of an employee deciding to leave their company. Either they were lured by an increase in their compensation, or, their family situation, such as maternity matters, illness, relocation, or other matters, impacted their decision.

## Decency

The concept of a decency quotient (DQ) is twofold.[24] First, employees seek this from their workplace and leadership as a way to discern the basis of a career decision. It is what attracts employees to want to join a company and ultimately what leads them to want to stay. Secondly, from a leadership perspective, having a high DQ focuses your attention on having a genuine desire to do right by others with honesty, kindness, and integrity.

For today's leaders, attributes such as empathy, listening skills, emotional intelligence, and decency are more critical than ever. They must be exercised like a muscle, practiced, and cultivated every day. These skills are crucial in managing and navigating the intricate issues of differing opinions, cultures, and emotions. As I have said so frequently in my talks around the world, to truly strive for diversity, inclusion, and equity in the workforce, decency has to be at its heart. Decency is the differentiator, and as a concept is simple, concise, and universal.

With the growing presence and economic power of women, the workplace of today is one of new attitudes, new concerns, and new expectations. And the person who leads them must have the right set of intrapersonal and interpersonal skills to do so.

Today, the premium is not on organizational management, but people management. Taking a talented, highly motivated, diverse workforce and blending them into high-performance teams that challenge, collaborate, and innovate. Their motivation, feeling like they belong, are valued, challenged, understood, and compensated commensurate with their value. These are the secrets of leadership success today, which can be simplified into a basic human quality that resides in us all, the decency quotient.

So, when asked, why do people leave companies? The answer is complex yet remarkably simple. It is not having the common denominator of inclusion, belonging and decency.

# CHAPTER 4

## Flexibility and the Evolution of Empathy

*"If you judge people, you have no time to love them."*
*– Mother Theresa*

When I transitioned careers from the pharmaceutical industry to motherhood, not only was I stretched more than ever before both physically and emotionally, but my arsenal of professional skillsets was also expanding.

I had always thought of myself as being a decent communicator, whether presenting at a meeting or drafting a companywide memo. However, it wasn't until I became a mother that I began to scratch the surface of understanding what being an effective communicator actually meant. When my children were very young, their communication cues were different pitches of cries or body movements. Through listening, observing, and being very patient, I would quickly learn to read these cues and adapt to their needs. I had now developed a heightened sense of empathy, become a better listener and, best of all, I learned how to negotiate with my children. I was more confident, empathic, and experienced as a result.

## The Significance of Empathy

From the late 1990s, leadership effectiveness was no longer just about task management; it's also about people management. Leadership was becoming less about directing and controlling, and more about negotiating and collaborating. As the concept of emotional intelligence—or being aware of yours and other's emotions—gained in popularity, the measurement of one's emotional intelligence, the emotional quotient, or EQ, came to be. Just as we had the IQ to measure our intelligence, we now had a comparable assessment to measure our emotional intelligence.

Thus, a new mantra was added to the leadership domain. But what are the core skills that enable emotional intelligence? This is where the concept of empathy becomes critical, and like any skill, empathy is one that must be practiced, cultivated, and valued.

These intra- and interpersonal skills inherent in emotional intelligence are many, such as the sensitivity, listening, and observational skills. But the foremost skill in the practice of emotional intelligence is empathy. Simply stated, empathy is the ability to understand or feel what another individual is experiencing. It is the cornerstone of EI.

While we may not have undergone the same experience as someone else, we can certainly still empathize with what they may be feeling. For example, I may not be brand new to an organization, but having transitioned to working from home remotely during the COVID pandemic of 2020/2021, I can certainly empathize with a new employee and the feeling of uncertainty or confusion.

## Empathy should unite, not divide

Author Brené Brown writes: "Empathy fuels connections, whereas sympathy drives disconnection."[25]

Empathy should not be confused with sympathy. One is being proactive, whilst the other is pitying. Another way of thinking about this would be posting a single Black post on social media demonstrating solidarity with the Black Lives Movement. Although this may raise awareness of a very important event, what this actually does, however, is show pity, without anything coming of it. If instead of posting on social media, people instead were asked to volunteer their time and resources to say, a local inner-city school, or ask their children to become pen pals with and write letters to children in these schools, that is showing empathy and understanding from both sides. One is taking action, showing accountability, and actually doing something, whereas the other gets you likes on social media.

There is a danger that although the focus on racial equality and the important work of the Black Lives Matter movement is long overdue, it could also send the message of gender equality as being "done." Not only does this omit the nuances of intersectionality and the specific challenges faced by Black or other minority group women, it risks undoing years of progress, especially as women, especially women of color, who are more likely to have been laid off, furloughed, or quit their jobs during the 2020/2021 pandemic.[26]

So as leaders trying to build a culture of decency and inclusion, this is actually a wake-up call for anyone who may not yet have grasped how precarious the situation is for women's careers right now. While focusing on one minority group, do not neglect another. As McKinsey[27] reports, with the pandemic intensifying pressures that women already face, more than one in four is now contemplating downshifting their careers or leaving the workforce completely due to the lack of resources and unequal split of household responsibilities.

So empathy not only helps us better understand another's feelings or circumstances, it is the bridge to establishing a much closer relationship with that individual. Empathy has been defined as an essential ingredient in enabling us to gain better insights, make better decisions, resolve conflicts, and collaborate with others. At the same time, we are forging closer, more meaningful relationships.

As we interact with others, empathy begins when we listen intently to what is being said in addition to taking the time to reflect on questions such as "What would I do if I were in that situation?" or "How would I feel if that had happened to me?"

For example, noticing which employees may need a flexible-work arrangement, or listening to what all employees are saying and assuming a shared (connected) goal of creating value and success, to be open to figuring out a workable solution.

It is these types of questions that spawned the expression "walk a mile in my shoes." It is also those questions that help us acknowledge and overcome one of the deadliest sins in how we perceive or judge another.

The objective is not to feel sorry for the individual (sympathy), but to better understand what their state of mind must be both mentally and emotionally. That is the starting point for truly engaging another individual.

## Empathy is key to successful corporate culture

Diversity and inclusion in the workforce is the single most talked-about theme in business today, with empathy being at the heart of both.

Practicing empathy requires a commitment on behalf of corporate leaders to open-mindedness, diversity, flexibility, trust, and accountability. For this to work though, employees have to practice and commit to empathy in return.

Corporations have to be aware that they aren't seeing or hearing all that they could about their workforce. And what they aren't seeing or hearing is costing them talent. Organizations with diverse leadership are perceived as more empathetic—a statement with which seventy-five percent of employees and ninety percent of CEOs and HR professionals agree. From the same study,[28] *The 2019 State of Workplace Empathy Study: The Competitive Edge Leaders are Missing*: "Empathy matters more than ever, and without it, you're falling behind," notes that eighty-five percent of employees said that empathy results from leadership implementing strategies to increase diversity and inclusion.

In the 2019 study by Businesssolver,[29] a benefits technology company, ninety-one percent of CEOs believed that empathy is directly linked to a company's financial performance, while ninety-three percent of employees say they're more likely to stay with an empathetic employer. This is relevant, because while ninety-two percent of CEOs say their organization is empathetic, in reality, only seventy-two percent of employees agree. Interestingly, the study finds that employees overwhelmingly (ninety-three percent) say that they're more likely to stay with an empathetic employer and would even work longer hours to stay with one (seventy-eight percent). Add to this that eighty percent of millennials and sixty-six percent of Baby Boomers noted that they would leave their current job if their office became less empathetic.

My hours at Goldman were often very long, but I loved the culture and sense of belonging in the teams I was part of, and that bond far outweighed the fact I spent most of my waking hours in the office. It also outweighed perks. True, office "perks" are a nice to have, but if I didn't jibe with the company culture or team ethics, perks wouldn't have mattered at all. On the contrary, I left the pharmaceutical industry after I felt my manager wasn't being empathic to planning next steps appropriately after I announced I was pregnant.

It's worth remembering that miscommunication and lack of empathy comes from not knowing. It can be a simple lack of education in a certain area that can cause conscious or unconscious biases, misunderstandings, leading to discrimination and non-inclusive behavioral patterns. For example, it is common to have heard woes about how men at work don't understand women and vice versa. As with any leadership or life issue, the best way to deal with this is to problem solve and hit the nail on the head, so to speak. We hear often that female employees that take maternity leave feel from their colleagues—both men and women—that maternity leave is basically a vacation from work. Or comparable to garden leave where you sit on the proverbial "beach" for some months. So how to resolve this? Well, you can start talking with coworkers about any differences between garden leave or vacation and maternity leave. Then, practice your script and present your findings. You could even use role playing as an example. In such ways, so many other situations can start to be tackled.

When people feel recognized and valued, they thrive. In simple terms, recognition is about what people do; appreciation is about who they are. This is nicely denoted in a *Harvard Business Review*[30] *article on this very topic.*

*Leaders can drive the empathy evolution by understanding what employees value in terms of benefits and workplace "perks." Ninety-five percent of employees want an employer who cares about their physical and mental health and empowers them with flexibility—for both work location and schedule. Ironically, work perks like happy hours, free food, pet adoption services, and spa services don't hit the mark for most employees, even though, according to Businesssolver's 2017 study,*[31] *many CEOs think those are what employees want.*

## Flexibility

Company leaders must empower their workforce to make good judgment calls regarding flexible working arrangements, by actively training them in key skills specific to making a flexible working arrangement succeed for the individual, their manager, and the company.

Flexible working arrangements have not only proven to be more family-friendly, but studies show that offering employees a greater lifework balance reduces companies' operational and capital expenditures, leading to gains in performance and productivity.

Today's reality is a company's flexibility, which must also encompass the flexibility for employees who take a temporary absence from the workplace, for whatever reason. How companies address this growing issue is no different from how they accommodate the issues of flexible hours or work-at-home practices.

Today, corporations are embracing flexibility policies that accommodate the needs of employees who say their loyalty to a firm often depends on whether a policy is in place. In an IWG Global Workspace Survey[32] more than a third of the prospective employees interviewed stated that flexible working conditions were more important to them than compensation, title, or being given a more prestigious role in the company.

There's also a problem with trust. A survey by the Family and Work Institute found that two out of five people worry about using the flexibility their employers offer, fearing it could jeopardize their jobs. People also fear taking paid family leave in the first place, a major Pew survey[33] found recently.

At the same time, seventy-eight percent of businesses believe offering flexible working enables them to expand their talent pool. More than a third of people would say that flexible working is so important and that they would prioritize it over having a more prestigious role (thirty-five percent). Sixty-three percent of the companies surveyed report at least a twenty-one percent improvement in productivity because of flexible working.

In another study[34] of prospective employees, forty-one percent of the respondents said they would take a ten percent cut for a company that cared more about employee wellness. Eighty percent of the respondents said they would be more loyal to their employer if it offered job flexibility, and more than half said they have attempted to negotiate flexible working conditions with their employer. Their study at a Fortune 500 company showed that workers who participated in a pilot work flexibility program voiced higher levels of job satisfaction and reduced levels of burnout and psychological stress than employees who worked for the same company but did not participate. A year later, and subsequently three years out, employees in the experimental group reported less interest in leaving the organization than those in the control group.

Areas where managers can deepen their awareness into actionable decisions with positive impact include:

- Lifework Balance

    o Examples: company sponsored seminars or access to experts on sleep, nutrition; discounted gym memberships; mandatory vacation days; company support for participating in flexible work or health related programs.

- Life-Changing Moments

    o Deeper understanding of what these could encompass: a birth, a death, an accident, a trauma, a physical illness, a mental illness, etc. How to recognize them and address them thoughtfully.

- How to Manage a Returning Employee

  - ○ Companies commit to a template for general situations, adaptable for common ones, and prepare managers well ahead of time on how to best welcome back an employee whose life circumstances have changed and, as a result, may require a changed schedule or working arrangement. How to communicate through that, make it work with the employee, and then to monitor it and measure success.

- Managing the New Team Dynamic

  - ○ Team members of a newly returned employee who may have a different working arrangement due to a change in circumstances may themselves need help in processing, accepting and adjusting to change. Managers should be trained on how to keep the team dynamic focused on results and empathy, the undercurrent point being that an unexpected circumstance could occur to any one of them and they would be granted the same level of understanding and support.

Flexibility not only makes workers happier and healthier but makes workforces more productive.

## The Emerging Workplace

Employees' expectations about empathetic behaviors are evolving as we experience an increasingly diverse workforce. For example, Baby Boomers are reaching retirement, Gen X'ers and Millennials are balancing family responsibilities of both children and parents, while Gen Z's are grappling with education costs, to name only a few. Keeping up with the changing times requires organizations to be attuned to their different needs. With so many competing and varied forces affecting workers, it makes sense that empathy resonates as a foundational workplace value.

Further, they care more about the social and environmental implications of their work. For this new wave of workers, whether a military veteran returning to civilian work, women and other minority groups, including LGBTQIA+, people with chronic illnesses or recovering from major traumas or any other group of individuals who may have experienced workplace obstacles, a multicultural workforce is becoming a way of life.

In this generation of workers, men have become more engaged in parental roles than any previous generation. They are more inclined to stay home from work when a baby becomes sick or other emergency and are more inclined to take a leave of absence to support the transition of a new baby into their family. We see increasing numbers of stay-at-home dads around the world, as partners go to the office to support their families. In contrast to previous generations who lived to work, this new wave of workers and entrepreneurs work to live.

This dramatic transformation in the workplace has been enabled in large part by technology and by the growing presence and economic power of women. Consider the contrast of the work environment of your parents, even as recently as ten years ago. Previous generations of workers had no time to worry about or contemplate social or environmental issues. They were too busy earning a living for their family. Issues, such as the "Me too" movement, or global warming, or the many other social issues of the day, would have been viewed as a distraction that interfered with the economic issues of surviving and progressing.

The workplace of today is one of new attitudes, new concerns, and new expectations. And the person who leads them must have the right set of intra- and interpersonal skills to do so.

Understanding privilege, leading with decency, and being a good coworker or ally are fundamental to a successful leadership culture. For example, consider a male manager. Although he may have empathy toward female coworkers because he may have a wife, a daughter, or grew up with a sister or had a mother that went to the office, that doesn't mean he will fully understand what women truly experience (and vice versa, of course): walking with keys between your fingers in the dark; being conscious of how you dress; enduring sexism whether it is being at the brunt of the banter or hearing it elsewhere. As a manager, and a leader, it is important to listen to and acknowledge any issues that your female employees may bring up. This is where you would lead with decency, to genuinely make sure that your employee is being heard, included, and treated fairly.

All levels of employees should be exposed to flexible thinking and training as part of their career development, and senior level executives should be especially visible in supporting, participating, and communicating the importance of practicing empathy, where employee performance reviews should include an assessment of their level of intelligence, empathy and decency combined. In other words all this would be a measurement of their decency quotient.

**Five Ways to Practice Empathy and Decency:**

1. Reach out to an employee who's new to the company or the team and inquire how they're doing, and the biggest challenge they've faced since joining, or the biggest misconception they had regarding the company (team).

2. Have a "culture" event, whether during a break or at an offsite meeting, and challenge team members to tell something others may not know about their culture (whether from a different country or a different region of the country).

3. Tell a member of the team your first impression of them when you first met them, or when they first joined.

4. Play the "If I were the CEO game." Have each person complete the sentence, "If I were the CEO, I would _____."

5. Celebrate the holidays of the members of your team, from different countries, and have them explain the origins and the significance of the holiday.

A more diverse workplace is a more empathetic one. A more empathetic workplace is a more flexible one, and a more flexible workplace is one where employees want to work, stay, and grow.

There was a time in our history when employers held all the cards in the workplace. They defined the jobs workers could apply for. They defined what those jobs would consist of. They decided the compensation, the terms, and the standards by which those jobs should and must be performed. Those times are no longer.

Today, the premium is not on organizational management, but people management. Taking a talented, highly motivated, diverse workforce, and blending it into several high-performance teams that challenge, collaborate, and innovate, while feeling like they belong, are valued, challenged, understood, compensated fairly, and commensurate with their value. When overwhelmed by the many complexities of today's organizations—its structure, technologies, people, and competitors—there is one simple attribute that ultimately resides in us all: the decency quotient.

# CHAPTER 5

## Curating a Culture of Decency: Top Down

*"The most practical kind of leadership is the leadership of decency."*
*– Theodore Roosevelt*

After my decade at Goldman Sachs, I was branded by fellow Goldmanites as being "Goldmanized." This was a phrase that meant the culture and way of doing things was now a part of me. And this was so true. Whether in the pharmaceutical industry, motherhood, or entrepreneurship, there are ways I think, take action, do things, that are the muscle memory, all things that I can trace back to the culture at Goldman. Now, to examine this word in this context, culture is the feeling of a company you get when you walk into a building or into a room. It is the DNA of the firm's way of doing things. It is a competitive advantage, difficult to replicate, and a strong factor in whether employees choose to apply to or stay in a company.

**The evolution of leadership cultures**
Workplace cultures have changed more in the last century with women in the workforce, increased awareness, and acceptance of different working customs and cultures through globalization, and the realization that workplace culture has a direct impact on the

bottom line. However, the evolution of workplace culture has not kept pace with the awareness of the facts that can help or hinder workplace success. In a 2016 study by Deloitte,[35] eighty-six percent of companies rate work culture as a top priority, with ninety-five percent of job seekers citing culture as more important than compensation. Likewise, ninety-one percent of hiring managers said a candidate's fit with the company culture is equally or more important than applicable skills and experience. A paycheck, the study found, shows up in your bank account once, maybe twice a month, but a company's culture lives with the employee every day.

In a report by Oracle,[36] the top four values observed were trust, engagement, energy, and focus.

With different times came different leadership styles.

For starters, a company's culture is not unlike the culture of your community or your country. It comprises a montage of laws, policies, beliefs, opinions, and ultimately, behaviors and practices. Companies attempt to shape and define their cultures through a collection of stated values and beliefs. Its actual culture, however, is defined by the behaviors of its leaders, and in turn, its workforce. A company's culture is determined by how managers engage employees, how employees engage one another, and how they collectively engage their customers. It is how employees celebrate each other's victories and support each other in times of failure or disappointment.

By the time I had taken a position with Goldman Sachs, the international banking and trading firm enjoyed a culture as a conservative, traditionally male-dominated firm, steeped in a rich history of success. Though the firm was founded and headquartered in the US, it was founded by a Bavarian immigrant whose strong conservative values could still be felt in the company one hundred and fifty years later. The firm's culture was defined by characteristics such as dedication, teamwork, and profits, which translated into long workweeks and strong accountability.

During my time with the firm, it was making significant efforts to modify its culture to attract a more diverse workforce and adapt its culture to the changing times. Though the firm was deeply entrenched in its rich history and male-dominated culture, it was not immune to the societal changes that were shaping its workforce.

So, how does a company like my alma mater, Goldman, or any other company that is entrenched in its values and its long-term history of success, reshape its culture to remain competitive in a world of growing diversity?

To answer that question, a little historical context is needed to demonstrate just how far those companies have had to go in modifying their cultures. In the past fifty years, the make-up of the workforce of traditional western corporations has evolved from:

Traditionally white males, to

White males, plus people of color, to

White males, plus people of color, plus females, to

White males, plus people of color, plus females, plus disabled, to

White males, plus people of color, plus females, plus disabled, plus sexual orientation, to

White males, plus people of color, plus females, plus disabled, plus sexual orientation, plus gender identification, to

White males, plus people of color, plus females, plus disabled, plus sexual orientation, plus gender identification, plus returning workers.

Navigating those changes and appealing to an increasingly diverse workforce is more than simply complying with new employment laws or changing the mission statement or the company's stated values and hiring practices.

Changing the talk is one thing; walking that talk, however, is something else.

## Corporate cultures

An exercise to practice is jotting down words that would describe your current corporate culture, as well as what your ideal workplace environment would be. Do you come up with words like stimulating, inviting, embracing, and competitive yet rewarding? Or do words like drab, humdrum, backstabbing, or toxic creep in?

A company's culture, and how that culture is reflected in its workforce, is a major factor in determining its success or failure. In a 2019 report[37] by the Society of Human Resources Management (SHRM), the organization published a study that found a direct correlation between companies that are viewed as having a tension-filled or toxic work culture and its bottom-line performance. The study found tangible differences in performance metrics, including drops in productivity, deterioration of employee well-being, and loss of profits. The study concluded that companies that displayed a healthier, more diverse and inclusive culture, created a clear competitive advantage.

**Understanding decency**
When I first entered the world of finance in the early 2000s, the most critical leadership quality my peers and I were measured against was the intelligence quotient, or IQ. As I progressed into the next decade, the emotional quotient, or EQ, became the prime focus. Although these are indeed key attributes in leadership development, the one trait that encapsulates all the people-friendly qualities that your employees, clients, and shareholders look for in their leaders boils down to one thing: whether you are a decent person.

The concept of a decency quotient (DQ) is twofold. First, employees seek this from their workplace and leadership to ultimately decide on whether to go with this or that employer. It is what attracts employees to want to join a company, and ultimately what leads them to want to stay. Secondly, from a leadership perspective, having a high DQ focuses your attention on having a genuine desire in doing right by others, thus ensuring everyone feels respected and valued. It is ultimately the evolution of your IQ and EQ, and is grounded in the key measurements of honesty, kindness, and integrity.

For today's leaders, attributes such as empathy, benevolence, listening skills, emotional intelligence, and decency are more critical than ever. They must be exercised like a muscle, practiced and cultivated every day. These skills are crucial in managing and navigating the intricate issues of differing opinions, cultures, and emotions. As I have said so frequently in my talks around the world, to truly strive for diversity, inclusion, and equity in the workforce, decency has to be at its heart. Decency is the differentiator, and as a concept is simple, concise, and universal.

With the growing presence and economic power of women, the workplace of today is one of new attitudes, new concerns, and new expectations. And the person who leads them must have the right set of intrapersonal and interpersonal skills to do so.

Thus, the decency quotient is getting more recognition. Whether from the CEO of Mastercard, Ajay Banga; or the Dean of the Fuqua School of Business at Duke University, Bill Boulding, decency is being recognized as the missing cog of three critical attributes for workers and leaders, namely IQ, EQ, and DQ.

Today, the premium is not on organizational management, but people management. Taking a talented, highly motivated, diverse workforce and blending them into high-performance teams that challenge, collaborate, and innovate. Whether employees feel marginalized for gender, social or cultural backgrounds, it is ultimately decency that will transcend these issues. Their motivation, feeling like they belong, are valued, challenged, understood, and compensated fairly that's commensurate with their value. These are the secrets of leadership success today, which can be simplified into a basic human quality that resides in us all, the decency quotient.

The word says it all. Decency. As a concept it is so simple, so concise, and should form the foundation of leadership structures. So, why then don't all corporate cultures measure this and benchmark for the level of DQ in leaders? It is because we are still evolving to get to this point. Decency was not always viewed to be the core attribute of leadership it is becoming in organizations today.

So just how do you curate a culture of decency?

**Broaden your perspective**

Earlier I shared the story of my encounter with an attendee at a women's networking event in New York City, where I donned a nametag with the acronym "SAHM" written on it, and when I explained this stood for "Stay at Home Mother" she turned her back and walked away.

My immediate thought was that the woman didn't want to be associated with someone who was "just a mum." However, my curiosity prompted me to follow the woman and ask why she responded that way.

To my surprise, she was taken aback and genuinely embarrassed. Firstly, as I had called her out, and secondly, as she had no idea that she reacted that way. We started chatting. It turned out that she only planned on being at the event for a short while and wanted to meet as many people from the finance industry as possible. So when she learned my nametag didn't stand for a financial institution, she quickly moved on to speed network with someone else.

As with anything in life, there are two sides of the coin, with even more iterations of logical outcomes whereas from my perspective I had initially thought that this woman had an issue with my current career choice of motherhood. From her perspective she was just trying to be efficient with her time. Granted, her delivery and body language could have done with some significant finessing, but this shows how easily misunderstandings can cause rifts and influence mindsets.

Especially if you are in a leadership position and your focus is in curating a culture of success, it is imperative to be as openminded, understanding, and neutral as possible.

**Honesty and openness breeds trust, and in turn loyalty...**
If you are a leader, then you have a responsibility to educate, and to not sensor information. Workplace culture can be discriminatory. For example, in a leadership's drive to "find the right fit," you are inherently requesting those employees in charge of hiring new talent, to source others who are more like them, in terms of mind frame, personality, and background. So actively moving away from the standard narrative takes stepping out of the comfort zone of your immediate hiring circle and venturing to pastures richer and more diverse.

And when doing so, understand the type of diverse environment you are trying to create, and why. By enabling employees of various backgrounds to come together, you will encourage a healthy work environment where everyone feels able to communicate effectively, and feel valued for who they are and what they bring to their team.

So, when curating your leadership culture top down, or bottom up, don't sensor your history, whether it's the past of your company, leadership, or educational materials. As times move ahead, disagree you may, but hiding from the past rather than acknowledging and moving forward won't build trust in the long run.

Another way to think about this is by restricting access to period fiction or history books. To do so means inadvertently hiding rather than acknowledging, learning from and moving forward. By trying to wipe people's minds of a different era, you are stopping education and an understanding of diversity and inclusion. Take the movie made about the life of Mahatma Gandhi which was released in the UK in the 1980s. Imagine if the script was pulled before the movie could even have been made. Or the movie was pulled because of the racially charged language. I remember my parents would tell me when they went to watch the premiere in London, there were British people in the theater in silence. They wept during the movie. From that comes change. From that education comes empathy and understanding. Growing up in racist Britain in the 1980s, the movie release actually brought up a different emotion in those who watched it.

Similarly, if a period novel had been written getting into the era of racial tension, be it Mark Twain's *Adventures of Huckleberry Finn* or Laura Ingalls Wilder's *Little House on the Prairie*, banning the book or revoking an award isn't a case of educating the public. After all, of those who have read the books or watched the movies, how many people have felt educated about the past and therefore now feel more empowered to make informed and empathic decisions in the future?

Trust is a foundational tenet that is hard to earn—and easy to lose when violated. Companies can have an excellent cultural reputation that can be destroyed overnight by a simple violation of trust by management. Conversely, a courageous act of trustworthiness can recover the most difficult of circumstances. A question to ask yourself is whether the owners, leaders, and hiring managers of an organization can be trusted to actually do what they say and to say what they do. Further, what do they do to acknowledge and rectify any deeds of mistrust downstream in the organization?

Aaron Feuerstein was the CEO of Malden Mills, a textile mill in Lawrence, Massachusetts. In 1995 a fire destroyed the mill that had employed some 3,200 people. Feuerstein could have taken the insurance money and moved his manufacturing overseas. At the age of seventy, he also had the option of retiring. Instead, Feuerstein promised his workers that he would rebuild the mill and save their jobs, and he kept them on the payroll. Feuerstein's concern for his employees, despite the cost to himself, gained their trust.

When asked about his CEO's actions, an employee told a reporter, "When we needed him most, he was there for us. And for that reason, we are there for him."

Which brings us to the next foundational tenet cited in the aforementioned Oracle report.

## Communications and listening

Listen before you speak and know and acknowledge that you don't always know. Take the time to understand both sides before passing comment. There's a reason or foundation for people having their viewpoints, stemming from their education, upbringing, childhood memories, or interpretation of something. Don't try to change someone's views, but instead take a step back to listen first, empathize with their "why," then show acknowledgment and understanding. Acknowledging another viewpoint shows respect and doesn't mean that you have to agree by any means. Once you acknowledge another's view, you can have your turn in explaining yours too.

For most people, the art of negotiation is practiced over time, rather than a skill you are born with. Granted, there are some people who seem to do this more naturally than others. To make change happen, you need empathy and understanding of the alternate viewpoint first. If you meet someone with resistance, you'll get resistance back.

For example, if I want my kids to do a certain task, experience has shown that being nice to them and giving them compliments rather than berating them is way more effective. If I want my kids to clean up their room, shouting at them to do it often delays the process and stresses both of us more. However, by taking the time to acknowledge and hear about what they have built or been working on in a calm and encouraging manner engages them. Then, a reminder of our clean-up rule at the end of playtime—perhaps snapping a quick picture to store the memory and to entice them to think of new ideas for the next clean-up session—is more likely to not just get the task done for next time, it will build rapport and understanding too.

Transferred into the workplace, these behaviors demonstrate executive management is walking the talk. Seeing these values practiced, in action, and training and empowering people on how to do so, influences the entire organization.

Curating a workplace culture takes into account the needs of many to achieve an ultimate shared goal of value creation, stemming from a foundation of security, safety, respect, trust, engagement, and support. The value of creating a positive culture for all employees, inclusive of those traditionally overlooked or unleveraged for a variety of reasons is inarguable: people are happier and more productive for being valued and attended to. In turn, they create a virtuous circle of support for other employees, leading to a flexible and welcoming company-wide culture of high productivity, trust, and retention, which are all deliverables that can also be tracked as measurements of success.

## Engagement...

Employee engagement is perhaps the most discernable and evidentiary indicator of a positive corporate culture. It is the measure of how much an employee is actively involved in his or her work and devoted to the success of the company.

Dr. Diane Hamilton, author, syndicated radio host and consultant, has written extensively on the topic of engagement. She says, "You will hear two common terms from employees who are highly engaged with their company: 'comfortable' and 'representation.'"

To think of the issue of comfortable is all encompassing for all employees, and irrespective of their gender, race or identification, they feel a genuine sense of belonging, whether you are a white male manager or a new joiner who has just moved from another country and is still adjusting to local dialects and customs.

By representation, we mean the company's makeup, and whether its organizational structure accurately reflects the diverse makeup of the communities served, and the communities' diverse customs and influences as a whole.

When gauging company culture, our value system, or the seven-second trigger[38] also referred to as unconscious bias, is naturally preset to look for other coworkers that look like us (or have had similar experiences), both in the grassroots team level as well as in positions of significance. Companies are not expected to capture the entire spectrum of the workforce mosaic in their hiring and promotion practices. They are expected, however, to openly embrace and reflect genuine diversity in those practices.

Having a management team or a board of directors exclusively made up of all white males is just as bad as a team with token representation or "the diversity hire." Employees can quickly tell the difference between a company that takes a genuine approach to diversity, and one that engages in tokenism in its hiring and promotion practices.

**True commitment means walking the talk...**
Too many times we see corporations lead great marketing campaigns with diverse looking employees showcased on billboards and other company promotions. However, time and time again, we have seen and heard that under the surface, the reality of these organizations is indeed very different, so much so that teams and individuals have often been left divided because of a lack of empathy, understanding,

and efforts in creating a truly diverse and inclusive workforce. In 2019, the Business Roundtable, an association of over one hundred and eighty chief executive officers of America's leading companies, concluded that the most immediate path toward sustained growth and profitability is, as can be expected, through its employees.

The CEOs issued a paper titled "Investing in our Employees," and it talks about fair compensation, employee support, and consistent training and education in order to foster the desired environment of diversity and inclusion, dignity, and respect. If management pledged to commit to their employee well-being as much as they did profits, then company culture could really change for the better.

Holding a corporation accountable for its commitment to its values is key therefore in measuring its willingness to "walk the talk." Patagonia founder, Yvon Chouinard, wrote a book titled *Let My People Go Surfing*, which served as the heart of the company's culture. Chouinard said the values of a company should not be limited to brochures, posters, or websites. They are for the people to experience day in and day out, on a sustained basis. Sustainability, in this context, relates to a company's work/life balance that engenders trust and a commitment of continually energizing and engaging employees.

It is this level of energy that goes beyond merely declaring or sponsoring a commitment to a company's values and its culture. It is the commitment to take responsibility and ownership for the culture, on a sustained basis.

Behaviors and traits that determine if executive management is walking the talk could include showcasing current company practices that have had positive feedback, such as Google's mandatory time off; Facebook's parental leave policies for both mothers and fathers (Mark Zuckerberg being a prime example of taking this leave); on-the-job training and reintegration training for employees coming back to the workforce after a career transition or leave; real retirement plans; flexible or remote work arrangements; better insurance coverage; and a voice in the running of the company.

## Curating your corporate culture

Curating a culture of diversity and inclusion is about harnessing the needs of many from diverse origins, to achieve a shared goal of productivity and value creation. That culture is anchored in a foundation of security, safety, respect, trust, engagement, and support for each employee, including those who are traditionally overlooked and unleveraged.

The result is a workforce of employees who are happier and more productive for being valued and attended to. In turn, they create a virtuous circle of support for other employees, leading to a flexible and welcoming company-wide culture of high productivity, trust, loyalty, and retention.

## Sustaining your corporate culture

Organizations, like people, change and evolve. Markets change, and in order to remain viable, companies must also adapt and change. The companies that thrive remain true to their values.

The oldest documented company in the world is a Japanese hot springs hotel, which has operated continuously for an astonishing 1,300 years. Nishiyama Onsen Keiunkan was founded in 705 A.D. to accommodate emperors, shoguns, and samurais who wish to bathe in the hot springs in the Yamanashi prefecture. The family-owned company's business model and its services, however, have changed with the times. But its culture has remained solidly consistent since its founding. Its secret? Through fifty-two generations, the company has been guided by three principles:

1. Put Your Employees First, Ahead of Growth and Shareholders: Making growth your priority, the original founder established, is an anathema to long term survival. Not only has the same family run the hotel for fifty-two generations, there are families among the staff who have held the same post for generations. That's why they run the business in the spirit of service, as a way to earn wages and protect the hotel, not as a way to profit.

2. Find Stability, but Be Flexible: The hotel business is one of the oldest in the world. In fact, most of the oldest businesses in the world are hotels, breweries, pubs, or restaurants. Finding an industry with relative stability is essential for building a company that lasts. The company has continuously modified its business model to accommodate market conditions, but its focus on its employees has remained constant.

3. Dedicate Yourself to Service: Of the 5,586 companies in the world older than two hundred years, a startling fifty-six percent of them, or 3,146 companies, are Japanese. Japan's unique dedication to service truly sets its companies apart from other countries. Japanese companies, to this day, are guided by a centuries old principle called "Giri Ninjo," which roughly translated, means "the loyal obligation of friendship." Intergenerational patronage takes the concept of the repeat customer to its extreme and it's the lifeblood of a company that's existed for centuries.

A company's business practices must continually evolve to remain competitive, from its value proposition to its methods and processes. Its culture, however, should be a constant.

**Wholistic workplace culture**
Most companies think of culture as top-down, where the vision, mission, and overall direction of the organization is shaped from C-suite leadership, and filters down. While this is quite true, this is something I challenge. When analyzing what shapes voices and how teams are led, there is a large influence stemming from the grassroots level—which is to say bottom-up instead. Typically, there are more junior employees than senior ones, and so themes, beliefs, and lifestyles of these fresher workforce members can influence the culture of the organization.

So although culture may initially come from top-down, where management infuses vision filters down the ranks, it is, however, bottom-up or grassroots culture that is the reality. Even with the best and most robust procedures in place, bottom-up culture isn't easy to document. It isn't something you can learn at work, but instead is the way of work. To succeed is to understand and adhere to the hidden rules of the playground.

# CHAPTER 6

## Rules of the Playground: Bottom Up

*"It is not the strongest of the species that survive, nor the most intelligent, but the one most responsive to change."*
*– Charles Darwin*

As children, we are not born recognizing differences in skin tone. Rather, it is something we are taught. Indeed, the first time I noticed I was darker was at school, when my friends used to call me names, throw away the contents of my lunchbox and motion me to eat grass. Apparently, this was done at the behest of their parents. Although being subjected to hurtful nicknames are a timeless rite of adolescence for all children, being a brown face in a predominantly white environment was the source of mine. That was my first memorable encounter with being different. At that time there was no avenue to post complaints of feeling mistreated or children being unkind; it was the rule of the jungle, or in my case the rules of the playground that dominated. However, rather than come home upset or downtrodden from hurtful remarks hurled at me from other children who didn't want a different-looking schoolfriend around them, I bottled up my emotions and just learned to "fit in" from an early age. I didn't ever feel like a foreigner though. This was my home and it was all I knew.

## Gut instinct

It was in those early childhood encounters that the teachings of my parents and the spirit of Uma, served me well. "What would Uma do in this situation?" I would ask myself. "How would she respond to juvenile, and sometimes hurtful, remarks?" We've all heard the lessons. "It's not what happens to you. It's how you respond to them."

And respond I did.

Although I didn't realize this at the time, ever since I was a little girl, I was blessed with the ability to think—and react—quickly. I still remember the time I was motioned to eat grass by a "friend" when I was five years old. As for what happened next, my gut told me that something didn't feel quite right, and so I asked the boy if he could demonstrate how to do this first, as I really didn't know how to do it. Others started to gather around, and soon joined in to ask the boy to eat grass. He didn't, and soon ran off. I think he got the point, as that was the last I had experienced "mean" behavior from that boy again.

Akin to the analogy of "learning to play dead," my experiences and those teachings have remained with me throughout my education, and into my career, in the UK, in the US, and later around the world. No matter the circumstance, that foundation continues to guide me. As a small child, being made to feel different was not always a pleasant experience; sometimes it was even painful. As I grew, however, I learned that being "different" is merely the starting point of discovering our "uniqueness." It's funny how those things we shun early in life become our most distinguishable attributes later on. The voices of my parents and the spirit of Uma were always there to remind me. How we deal with those encounters, I learned, ultimately determine who we are and who we become: from our beliefs about ourselves, about others, and how we view the world.

## Learning the rules

During the coronavirus pandemic of 2020, when there were in-person school days, I would often schedule my workday so that I could pick up my two children from their respective schools. My son's school dismisses into his playground. It was amazing to see the difference that in-person schooldays had on the overall mood of both my children in comparison to when they had remote-learning days. It was almost like they were different children altogether. Being social is a natural part of their being. Even though they both started new schools and met new friends for the first time, having the social interaction and the time to just run around the playground unfiltered allowed them to blossom and just be, well, themselves.

At pick up, I would observe in awe as the children—particularly mine—were running, jumping, sliding, navigating sharp scooter turns, and barely dodging each other as they played tag together. Some were narrowly missed; others would crash and fall. Some would react, others wouldn't. Regardless though, there was an unspoken understanding of playing by the rules—their rules. After all, have you ever wondered why some people are just naturally more "liked" than others? Perhaps they appear to have more social skills and an ability to fit right in. They understand the rules of the playground.

Ultimately, our younger years shape us. They define who we are, shape our views and are the foundation of our value system. Although there is a precedent that schools and teachers can set, there is also a survival instinct that pupils need to develop for themselves, exercised, and honed over time. Those are the rules of the playground, and they extend into our adult and working lives. If you don't play by the rules, you won't get far.

Even with the best school culture or workplace ethic, if you are not in tune with the social rules of your community—the proverbial playground—then you won't have the respect of your friends, peers, or later co-workers.

**Street smart**
With adjusting to the rules of the playground comes the ability to become street smart. Some of us have this instinct more naturally, while others learn from experience, with a combination of trial and error.

Put another way, being street smart also means knowing when to pick your battles, inadvertently being a great negotiator. As a child my mother often told me to befriend aggressors rather than stay away from them. I didn't understand what that meant until I grew up, but I certainly do with the work I do now. By not fearing and instead trying to mentally step into their shoes showed them I knew where they were coming from. I often found that showing this compassion and a level of understanding diffused the situation completely, and then I could present my viewpoint in a calm manner.

Although I may have had an opposing viewpoint in my head, I would appear very neutral, such that people from all sorts of backgrounds would open up to me. By understanding, rather than condoning, you can accept differences.

As I have shared on social media and my talks, as a woman and a minority I never want to be thought of as having been given a job or position just by virtue of being a woman or because of my Indian heritage. Above anything, I want to be respected as a peer, and as an integral member of the team, who is there because of my hard work, performance, dedication, and spirit. So when an inevitable issue pops up at work, this means the ability to pick your battles wisely, including with whom. At times, you have to simply let things roll off your back, in order to gain the respect and trust of your co-workers. You need to keep your eye on the prize so to speak. Do you want to ripple the stream with each stroke you take, or focus on your workplace goals, letting less significant issues wade by?

However, the current educational messaging and work construct encourages us to bring up anything we feel is unjust, whether it is an outcome we are unhappy with, or feeling of being treated unfairly. Although this may result in a disciplinary warning to a work peer, you also risk losing the camaraderie, respect, and trustworthiness of your colleagues. Point being, that by measuring carefully when to say something versus when not to, you are exercising the unspoken rules of your workplace playground. It doesn't mean you have to accept something or that you are letting someone get away with something they shouldn't have. You are merely prioritizing what and when. Think of the analogy here of one of Aesop's Fables, "The Boy Who Cried Wolf," wherein a false cry for attention could backfire, and you could end up being eaten by the corporate wolf you tried to avoid in the first instance.

Put another way, this is an act of resilience, combined with perseverance and grit. For inspiration, think of your favorite entrepreneur, athlete, sportsperson, or musician. I think of Steffi Graff, Usain Bolt, Roger Federer, Jennifer Lopez, and Hima Das. They are all champions, have laser focus, and the mentality of not giving up.

Similarly, we can all definitely learn a thing or two from entrepreneurs and parents—especially working mothers balancing family with professional life—about taking risk, grit, resilience, not giving up, and having the persistence to earn respect and build trust.

## Fitting in

"When in Rome, do as the Romans do."

Back in the early 2000s, Goldman's London equities division arranged a social to go go-carting. It was a fun evening with colleagues, and a great way to meet members of different teams. I had always loved driving but had never tried go-carting until then. First call of duty was to get changed into go-carting suits, listen to the safety briefing, and put helmets on before racing. Next ensued many qualifying rounds of heats. Competition was fierce and I still remember the roars of excitement from team members as we were getting ready to race. I was excited that I had made the final. Helmet on, thumbs up to teammates, and race. Flag down, I made the finish line. Results were in: I had won! I had not just won but claimed the new champion spot in the division. I was later informed that many were in disbelief that a female intern had beaten the reigning male partner on the floor, and no one knew who I was until I removed my helmet and got out of the car.

From that day onward, I was "in" in the club. I had earned my stripes. I was invited to poker tournaments on weekday evenings, took part in fantasy football leagues, invited to go golfing at weekends and just hang out at the pub post the market closing. I never finished my beer, and was known as the double parker, but, hey, that way OK and I was accepted for it.

I was officially part of the group, and now "protected" by my team. After I became an integral part of the team, our team outings wouldn't just consist of going for a pint next door after the markets closed. Through fitting in and accepting others for who they were and them accepting me, I have fond recollections of going out to lambada and salsa dance parties after work, because that was what I picked, and so the team came along. We all had a good time and shared the common goal of respect and acceptance.

Ultimately, I had to be good at my job and be easy to get along with. Those were the rules of the playground.

You may strive to be the best at your work or the most academic in your class at school, but ultimately, if you don't know the etiquette of using the monkey bars or when to get off the swing, or how to effectively dodge or integrate with other children running around you, then you may have a tough time.

This goes beyond cultures, race, ethnicity, identification, or gender. It is whether you have the social skills and are likeable or not. How you integrate with or get along with others. Yes, it is also up to how others welcome you into the conversation too, but whether you remain in the conversation may well be about likeability.

As a pupil at school or employee at work, you need to develop social skills, resilience, work hard and with honesty.

But what if you didn't know how to fit in? What if you were "that" child that did look different and have a different accent to everyone else? As with any new school or role, there is a probation period, where you will be scrutinized for everything and by everyone. Think of this as a trust-building exercise.

As an employer, while having the correct workplace culture, empathy, diversity, a sense of belonging, and decency tools are key, you also need to allow team bonding to occur, so that the rules of the "team" playground so to speak are also understood.

When you think of which teams have a successful dynamic, you can equate their performance and reputation according to a sports team or army operation. Each team member works together seamlessly. They are almost family. To compare this to a sports analogy for teamwork ethics, "If the going gets tough, then the tough gets going."

## A rebellious streak

Having experienced a decade in the corporate world, being front row and center in the lion's den so to speak, then coming out not just alive but thriving, I have observed successful colleagues, both women and men, especially the traits of established female leaders. I have also observed who gets "quartiled" or goes in the firing line at year-end review if their performance falls within the bottom quartile of their peer group.

Simply put, the rules for how to succeed on the trading floor are universal whether your background is from the corporate world, academia, marketing, science, government, and even in real life. These are the rules of the playground.

To start, don't strive for perfection. It's something women do a lot in order to outdo even ourselves. But if you let go just a little, relax your grip around the tennis racket, baseball, or rounders bat, they you are more likely to get a better shot. A lesson I learned as a new mother was to let go. When I relaxed the pressure, things got easier. When I trained myself to be OK with waiting a few minutes to pick something up or clean up a spill, everything became easier to deal with.

Next, ignore your achievements. Trophies, accolades, and all the other nice to haves you may have picked up in the past may form a gratifying feeling, but these are not sustainable or realistic. Because the reality of work is that you will not get rewarded or patted on the back for each little task you complete. You may not even reach a milestone to warrant a promotion in a few years, if at all. Therefore, don't strive for constant validation, as that is not an accurate measure of success in the working world. Instead, learn to be on that playground, and engage with your colleagues. By picking up on social cues and knowing when do give up your swing and go instead to the monkey bars, will serve you far more. Those that followed this find themselves getting invited to the "right" meetings, more often than not.

Be a bit rebellious and break some rules! If you have never been told off for getting into a bit of mischief, or ever experienced getting marked down on school tests, you won't know how to deal with the fear of authority talking to you when you later go on to have a job. When my own two children get into a bit of strife, I allow them to soak in the feelings themselves of their actions versus the consequences and how they react and respond to these situations. When they play cricket at the weekends, their coach sure doesn't give them a gold sticker for dropping the ball. They are learning resilience as a result of learning the rules of the playground in their everyday lives.

Children are naturally better at the rules of the playground and getting along with their peers when they are young. But this is often lost as they get older when their environment, peer group, and media influences take over. So we need to guide the next generation in maintaining their social awareness and open-mindedness so that it becomes a part of their future.

**Keep calm and carry on...**
Most companies think of culture as top-down, where the vision, mission, and overall direction of the organization is shaped from C-suite leadership and then filters down. However, it is actually the grassroots bottom-up culture that defines who will succeed or fail in an organization. If you fall down, it isn't just about getting back up, but how quickly can you get up again and dust yourself off. As a Brit, the phrase "Keep calm and carry on" comes to mind. When analyzing what actually shapes voices and how teams are led, there is a large influence stemming from the grassroots level, so bottom-up instead. Typically, there are more junior employees than senior ones and so themes, beliefs, and lifestyles of these fresher workforce members can influence the culture of not only organizations, but society overall.

Even with the best and most robust procedures in place, the bottom-up culture cannot be documented. It is not something you can learn at work, but instead is the way of work. To succeed, therefore, is to understand and adhere to the hidden rules of the playground.

# CHAPTER 7

# The Onus is on You: Accountability, Ownership, and Hard Work

*"Work and you'll get what you need; work harder
and you'll get what you want."*
*– Prabakaran Thirumalai*

I still remember the intensity of the dhoop incense burning in our family Namghar as part of the Assamese prayer ritual my mother performed each time a member of our family had an important event. This time the ceremony was performed to wish me success ahead of my first day at King's College London, where I was about to embark on my journey of mathematics and management.

During my time at King's, engaging in a chance conversation with a person I had never met, while waiting outside the entrance to a campus-wide career fair, ultimately started my decade-long journey in the world of finance. That friendly person happened to work at Goldman Sachs, and I happened to accept an invitation to "come and say hello" to other colleagues at the firm, which consequently lead to thirty-two interviews across five divisions and an eventual offer to join the summer analyst program in London.

Luck? Being at the right place at the right time? Perhaps an element of that. But what if the initial conversation I engaged in didn't go very far, or I put too much pressure on myself to impress the thirty-two interviewers? In that case, I wouldn't even have progressed to the next stages, let alone receive an offer.

Many people have asked me over the years how I define success. Usually as a follow up to the question of how I "survived" a decade in a cutthroat industry, which translates to how I became so successful at my work.

Well, it was a combination of not putting too much pressure on myself, so that I could really appreciate, absorb, and learn from the opportunities I was given; making time as well as taking the time to see what different team members did day to day; immersing myself into the role and team activities to build camaraderie; and most important, working sincerely and genuinely hard at the tasks and projects I was given. Experiencing the rules of the playground throughout my life helped me tremendously when recognizing social cues as well as how to prioritize and filter out must-do tasks from the optional (read compulsory) extras.

Ultimately, that experience and every experience in my life came through taking ownership, being accountable, rolling up my sleeves for some good old hard work, and certainly never taking anything for granted.

### Shared responsibility

There are many characteristics of the typical twenty-first century organization that our parents would faintly recognize. Businesses are more complex, processes are more automated, and systems are more multi-functional. The environment, as typified by an informality of meetings, interactions, and dress codes, are less restrictive. Most visible of all, current workforces imbibe a rich mosaic of colors, cultures, genders, nationalities, and perspectives.

There is another element in today's organizations, however, that may not be as visible, but far more instrumental, especially in those organizations that are more advanced and forward thinking in their practices, and that is the way employees are managed.

The hierarchical, top-down management style in combination with the grassroots culture-led bottom-up style, has given way to a management approach that is more open, collaborative, and with shared responsibilities. In the organization of the twenty-first century, workers have access to more information, and as a result, are more involved in those activities that were previously reserved for managers, such as planning, decision-making and the shaping of strategies. In this new organization, managers are viewed less as bosses, and rather as facilitators or coaches.

There is immense power in this new, more collaborative organization, where in theory, decisions can be made more quickly and closer to the source of the issue; conflicts can be resolved more easily; and strategies are more intelligence-based. This more open, collaborative approach to management has resulted in workers taking a much more active role in the burdens and challenges of leadership. As employees become more involved, they become more engaged. As they become more engaged in the day-to-day operational issues of the business, they take more responsibility, and hence, more ownership.

Leadership in this new, more enlightened organization, is less top down and dictatorial, and more collaborative. Collaborative leadership is just one of the several earmarks of this new collaboration between owner and employee. It is one of shared risks, shared responsibilities, and shared outcomes.

Further, this new collaboration is one of differing cultures, generations, appearances, and lifestyles. It is one that affords a healthier blending of work with family. Corporations are changing practices and policies, which once collided with the needs and concerns of its workers and their families, to now integrate and balance the two much more seamlessly.

There is a time-tested axiom in management: The more you are involved in the decision-making process, the more you are invested in the outcome. The more you are invested in the outcome, the more valuable you are to the organization. As workers participate more in management decisions, they become more valuable, and the more vital they are to the company's success, the more their voice is heard in how practices and policies are shaped.

## Keeping up pace

Business today moves at an unprecedented pace. It is more complex, with more diverse challenges, and competition is more intense. And the central ingredient required to survive and thrive amidst those changes is a fully engaged, talented workforce. This new collaboration between employer and worker has never been at more of a premium, and the practices required to attract and retain that talent have never been more complex.

Rather than taking the view that "we live to work," attitudes today are "we work to live."

## Retention is better for the bottom line

Companies have strong financial incentives to make their coaching and transition programs work and have started to coach new parents.[39] Ernst & Young, which recently expanded its policy to sixteen weeks of paid leave for all new parents, said it typically costs the firm 1.5 times an employee's salary to replace them. "When we train supervisors about how to be supportive, we see bottom-line effects for the company," said Leslie Hammer, an industrial organizational psychologist and professor at Oregon Health & Science University.[40] That might be from reduced turnover costs, less absenteeism, and fewer health expenses as well as workplace safety issues, even among employees working in offices, she said.

Given that retention trumps retraining, it seems in everyone's best interest therefore to retain employees, regardless of level of seniority or function performed, which can in turn affect a company's culture. Cultural norms need to be transparent, inclusive, responsive, and reasonable and need to receive both top-down and bottom-up support and engagement from all levels.

A combination of trust, engagement, consistency, and commitment to a supportive culture throughout the organization are requirements for this. The proof is in the pudding: Employees, managers, C-levels, and shareholders can all point to a bottom-line result of a culture that embraces flexible return policies and prioritizes diversity and inclusion, as can be seen in a recent International Workplace Group report.[41]

## Getting back to basics

If you didn't adhere to the dynamic rules of the playground during your formative years, you may find yourself having a harder time adjusting to social cues later in life whether personally or professionally. Going back to basics can help, as it is often the simplest things that can solve complex problems later.

The basic ingredients for this recipe are of course empathy, trust, and communication. Empathetic solutions are as diverse as people and workplaces. Each individual, whether an employee, manager, HR representative, or CEO can practice empathy and decency in a way that is authentic to themselves, the company, and the specific individual to whom they are communicating with.

In turn, the individual who is sharing their story must also be empathetic to the overarching needs, goals, and values of the person with whom they are speaking. The company has to meet its obligations, a manager their quarterly goals, and the employee, their contributions to those goals. Balancing empathy and awareness of a shared goal (success of an individual, department, corporation) is the shared value both parties agree upon when discussing and designing a flexible work plan.

An example that comes to mind for shared responsibility is parental leave, where managers receive ample resources and training on how to best welcome back mothers to the workforce, and similarly show increased acceptance and participation in fatherhood leave participation, where the United States lags. Even Twitter, which has extended its leave policy for all parents to up to twenty weeks of full pay, is offering formal coaching services to its managers. Similarly, there are many mental health benefits to all parts of the organization.

## Practice what you preach

One of my clients had called me up asking for advice, "I teach D&I, but for some reason score low on the empathy part of my personal yearend 360 review. I just don't get it." An HR director had just finished overseeing training on inclusivity and belonging. She had the dual task of recruiting for a role in one of her regional teams. I asked her about her hiring and communications process with candidates that her team decided to move forward with versus those that they were not going to pursue further. It so happened candidates progressing to future rounds would all receive an email and sometimes even a follow-up phone call, depending on level of seniority of the role. However, those candidates that were not going to advance further were not given the same courtesy. At times some would receive a very generic "thanks but no thanks" email, but not always, and with very little detail, if at all. By not responding, acknowledging or letting the candidate know, was even more demoralizing for a candidate that was perhaps already apprehensive about the job.

If you preach inclusivity and belonging but don't respond to emails and therefore choose not to apply this courtesy to all, you are being a hypocrite. If we revisit the concept of decency quotient, then your DQ would actually be quite low, as you are not demonstrating the genuine desire to do right by others.

It's the little things that count. Acknowledge an email. Companies don't like being ghosted, so why ghost others who have reached out to you? How can you preach D&I and not even respond to someone's email? Even a simple haven't heard anything but will let you know if I do, will do.

## Stop judging others

Harsh as it may sound, but unconscious bias training—at least the way it is delivered today—is ineffective. They are generally just a single training session, and other than highlight that we all have prejudices and that this is linked to our value system hence rooted in our upbringing thus stagnant, there is generally no proactive action after this "realization." Rather than walk away without addressing "what's next," instead we should be training groups on how not to jump to conclusions, how to view situations with a wider lens and with better listening and empathy. For example, how many of us irrespective of gender or race have feigned ignorance once upon a time on the train when a woman or with young children are clearly in need of a seat—our seat, the one we also paid good money for? Ultimately, perspective plays a huge part in this, plus our level of entitlement. Think of a pedestrian crossing and you are about to cross the road when a car or cyclist suddenly zooms past you almost chopping off your toe. On the contrary, if you are now the driver in a rush to pick up your kids from school and the light is still on yellow, you may now be beckoning pedestrians to wait their turn. Similarly, if you're trying to sleep on a flight and there's a crying baby down the aisle, imagine if you're the parent trying to console your infant who is battling motion sickness and cabin pressure changes for the first time. The list of real-life biases goes on.

## Perception is reality

Being immersed in diversity and inclusion initiatives for close to a quarter of a century, I have come to realize that the topic of diversity and inclusion isn't black or white by any means. Although there is no dearth of undeniable instances of gender, race, and cultural discrimination, this is not to be confused with instances of one's own perception of an outcome of a situation being attributed to gender or racial bias, whereas in actuality it is because of not completing a certain task on repeated occasions. If this realization isn't nipped in the bud at the outset, it can affect that employee's self-confidence, mental health, well-being and by extension, hard-work mentality.

Although companies such as Uma have the task of identifying, educating, and encouraging talented women and other minority groups to flourish in the workforce, in order to do so, it is imperative that those talented employees must not only learn to stand on their own two feet once they are in the workforce, they must also play by the rules of the playground in order to gain trust and acceptance by their colleagues in order to flourish and excel.

We most often see this advice given only to the hiring managers, senior leaders, and team training, but in order for true inclusion and belonging to occur, the onus is on both the new employee and the existing team to accept each other.

**The onus is on everyone**
Corporations, small- and mid-sized enterprises, the education system, policy makers, government and lawmaking bodies, conversations around the dinner table, and a patriarchy that is particularly prevalent in certain cultural backgrounds. The entire system is responsible, from conversations with friends and coworkers, to policy makers changing terminology and extending flexible benefits to both women and men for example.

Cost savings as well as a greater investment in the workforce, including training, family leave and other employee benefits, has placed a greater demand on employee retention, especially as this is inclusive to all employees who are all impacted, affected, or can affect a company's culture. Cultural norms need to be transparent, inclusive, responsive, and reasonable. They need to receive top-down and bottom-up support and engagement from all levels.

For example, employees may be aware of programs specific to their mental health, well-being, or life events, such as with flexibility or returning from leave, but in order for such programs to be effective, employees need to trust that participating in such programs won't hurt them in the short or long term with regard to career progression.

It is great that so many companies are putting programs in place to address workplace issues, especially those impacting parents returning to the workforce, and that employees are increasingly speaking up about what they see as crucial cultural adjustments in the workplace, as it keeps awareness high on all fronts. However, not only does the employer have to work on retaining their employees, but the employee also needs to feel enthused and as excited as they did with their very first day in the workforce to be able to learn, appreciate, and roll up their sleeves to get back in the thick of their careers once again.

In the work environment, it is the employee and not just the employer who needs to take ownership and responsibility for their own career paths. Everyone needs to be accountable for and acknowledge their actions. I have been called into organizations to "fix" employee situations, where in theory the messaging of speaking up and acting with confidence is promoted, but in practice, rather than having a foundation of empathy, listening, showing mutual respect and exercising decency toward peers, the employees were instead citing entitlement, arrogance, and playing victim as the source of peer-to-peer feuds. Far from an understanding team dynamic but a divisive environment that needed structured moderation sessions and a lot of un-training as well as re-training sessions.

There are situations to navigate in all of our lives, and knowing when, how, and with whom to pick your battles with is key. In a work environment, beyond genuine feelings of a sense of belonging and camaraderie, gaining trust from colleagues regardless of your gender, culture, ethnicity, or socioeconomic background will shine through when you show a genuine desire to work hard, learn, and absorb, rather than feel shortchanged in your role.

The education system also has an onus to help families as much as possible and not just rely on employers to provide help and childcare. Let's take childcare as an example. We often hear of fingers being pointed at corporations for not having onsite childcare solutions, whereas private schools or educational institutions that have rather generous endowment funds don't do enough to help. There needs to be flexibility and a willingness to help and solve these family issues all around.

Conversations around the dinner table with family, friends, and coworkers matter too. Taking the time to point out gender specific statements is a way of nipping generalizations in the bud before they can bloom into accepted statements. For example, clarification may be needed for the meaning of an old-fashioned statement such as "man of the house." There is an onus on society and household conversations to divide up household and parental responsibilities as fairly as possible. Step up as the "other" parent, and step in. Don't wait to be asked for help. After all, you're not doing anyone any favors by demonstrating your disinterest in helping.

## Don't play victim

When office politics or disagreements occur, there have been occasions when fingers get pointed toward gender or racial discrimination. Or to put this another way, allegations are presented of employees pulling the "race," "gender" or "diversity" card. While this may well be true, and if so, these concerns should be addressed to the maximum. Employers also have the tricky task of filtering out whether this is a discrimination issue or a perception one, and, if the latter is indeed the case, work on bringing them out of the perceived picked on, self-pity, or "victim" mentality. Instead, converting that to taking ownership of and pride for striving to be the very best that they can. In this case, focusing efforts on the wellness of the employee, and striving to bring out their confidence is key, which in turn can help with converting any prior issues to that of positive energy and working to their best in the circumstances as best they can.

## Make lemonade…

As the saying goes, when life gives you lemons, make lemonade. While we may not be able to control circumstances, nor what happens to you, we are all however, in control of our reactions. We choose our actions and decide what comes out of our mouths. We are the authors to our own destinies so to speak. When put at a crossroads in life, we can easily choose the easier path of familiarity, but think of the possibilities of choosing the path less traveled. The world is your oyster and only you will know what is happening next.

Being able to react with confidence while communicating calmly and negotiating your response is key. If you are more of an extrovert, then take the time to listen before jumping in to comment. Take a step back first, listen, repeat back what you have heard and acknowledge what you have heard (you don't have to agree), then move on or say your piece in a calm, kind, and not condescending manner.

## Don't let D&I policies discriminate

If an employer is rolling out fresh diversity and inclusion strategies or updating current hiring practices, they need to be mindful not to reverse discriminate while introducing these new policies.

Pigeonholing or stereotyping everyone is a classic example of where diversity becomes discriminatory. When I first relocated to New York from the UK, I would gravitate toward anyone with an English accent. However, when I went to a diversity networking event with others who had recently relocated to the city, I was randomly selected to be in a group of Indian people who had just moved from India. We had nothing in common; they were from mainland India, and I was from the UK. Even my heritage wasn't mainland India, as I am Assamese, so from the Seven Sisters region. So, although I got along with the group (I do love meeting new people), I had more in common with anyone with a British accent than a first-generation Indian. I would welcome messages of Merry Christmas, as I didn't grow up celebrating Diwali and would wish others Happy Bihu in the springtime, as that coincided with the Assamese new year. It still never ceases to amaze me how some diversity events still appear to discriminate by perceived race rather than cultural upbringing.

Hiring practices can also seem quite contradictory too. For example, a frequent woe reported by some of my clients, specifically those within the United States, is that whenever a position has been filled by a "diversity hire," the feedback circulated is that they were not fully qualified for the role at hand. While at first glimpse this may seem like a rather brash and uneducated statement, there is, however, a root problem that hasn't been addressed. For example, if ten board positions are to be filled, and seven of those are going to be by white males, then you may get a hundred or so applicants for those spots. However, for the three "diversity" hires, you may get just three referrals for the three spots and that's it. And on top of that, if the diversity hiring mandate had been to get a black person, a woman, and a male or female military veteran, an offer is made to the first person that fits the diversity mandate. However, in this scenario, the hiring "net" hasn't been thrown wide enough at all. It is no wonder that if the company hasn't made the effort to expand hiring outreach and so only receive a few applicants, the opportunity to hire qualified talent is being overlooked.

## Shared Visions

Sharing visions has led to a transformation, not only in the way employees are managed, but in the practices and policies regarding their work vis-à-vis their entire existence. This employee-employer synergy can be compared to many such other relationships, such as that of a parent-teacher-pupil at school; friendships that have transcended the tests of time; partnerships in marriage.

A heavy dose of communications, frequent check-ins, and adjustments always keeping the larger goal in sight. "Keep your eyes on the prize" is the overriding mantra. The right hand always knows what the left hand is doing and is prepared to step into the other's role when necessary. A successful marriage is built on a foundation of trust, one in which each partner knows that the other will do the right thing. Theirs is a partnership in which each enjoys the freedom to do what is right and shares the responsibility to uphold their end of the bargain.

By virtue of being given greater freedoms to execute their roles within organizations, employees are becoming more proactive in assuming greater responsibilities, and thus more engaged and invested in their companies.

Such successful partnerships are not hierarchical in nature, reflecting a dominant-subservient relationship, but instead have shared goals, tasks, responsibilities, and risks. Albeit a prescribed division of labor (for example, that of a teacher-pupil), depending on the nature and circumstances of the industry, there is also more flexibility, accountability and ownership.

Generally, roles and responsibilities in the workplace are not defined by gender in terms of "male" roles or "female" roles but by who is best suited to successfully execute the task, i.e., "Whose talents and circumstances will best position us to succeed?"

As an example, paternity leave exists in the United States for private companies, but most new fathers don't take it because it's not clear to do so. And their bosses have never taken it. It's just not a culture over here. But how is it a culture in Europe or New Zealand, for example? Granted, there is more of a government mandate for family leave in certain countries, but more importantly there is more of a family and shared-responsibility ethic. Having a culture where you can talk openly about sharing responsibilities from a family-unit perspective would ultimately help the entire company.

Organizations of the twenty-first century share these same characteristics. Each person is a player, and each person is a coach. Each has one eye affixed to their responsibilities, and the other to supporting their partner. Each participant is individually empowered to make certain commitments and requests, but once a flexible arrangement has been made to share the responsibility for the ultimate outcome they must trust in each other, the plan they devise, and the company's support.

Those categorizations and judgments may tell us the demographic makeup of our workforce but fail to tell us what is truly important to the success of the company: abilities to contribute, and to collaborate with others. Ultimately, the only two questions that matter should be: "How can you make our company better?" and "How can you make others around you better?"

Companies are slowly moving beyond the issues of categories, labels, and quotas to that place where we assess and judge applicants for their value and character, as opposed to solely by their résumé. We are slowly evolving to a place where companies are starting to value decency, and although we are making progress, we are not there yet.

There are still cultures and companies in certain countries that view males as superior to female employees. They question the abilities of those with gaps in their résumés, such as returning mothers or military veterans; judge performance based on facetime, rather than productivity or output; have policies and practices that fail to provide family leave; and fail to accommodate other work and family balance issues.

Every employee of an organization, ranging from the CEO to the most recent entry-level hire, ultimately wants the same thing: for the company they work for to succeed, to be part of creating and benefiting from that success, and for that to happen without undue stress or unfairness. In pursuit of that objective, we challenge company executives to enact and embrace policies that recognize and promote healthy work/family practices, including those that support maternity and paternity leave, and leverage technologies that promote virtual work practices, including location and time.

### Being accountable—inclusive leadership

An MBA graduate, Marcella Spatz, from the University of Business and International Studies in Geneva, Switzerland, was a new hire at the Swiss-based food company, Nestle Foods. She was to be a member of the marketing team in their bottled water division. In her third day on the job, she was asked to participate in a virtual conference with her team, many of whom she had never met. The group was launching a campaign to market their premium brands, Perrier and Poland Springs, to compete against standard bearers Coke and Pepsi.

After being introduced as the newest, and perhaps youngest employee in the group, Marcella settled back in her home office to listen and take in all she could on the call. Then a question arose regarding the task of getting market research on the competitive products in the country of Belgium. When the moderator asked who would like to lead the research effort, there was an extended silence on the call. It was then that the moderator asked, "What about you, Marcella? How would you like to get your feet wet on this campaign? We'll get two others from the group to help you gather the data."

In her third day with the company, and first day with her new group, many of whom she had never met, Marcella had gone from newcomer and observer, to taking a leadership role for a small group as part of a marketing campaign. Through hard work and perseverance, Marcella proved herself to be worthy of engaging in leadership discussions and decisions, and in turn, made her more invested in the success and bottom line of the company.

## Learnings

In companies around the world, there is an inherent tension in the relationships between leaders and their workforces. Just as workers settle into the processes and practices of the most recent changes, the threats of competition and new technologies force leaders to implement even newer changes.

Many of those changes are technical in nature. Others are changes of refined business practices or processes to achieve efficiencies. And yet, other changes are personnel related, such as employment practices or changes in compensation. Those are the most difficult type of organizational changes. Those are the type leaders have traditionally dreaded.

At Uma we are on a mission to change the cultural norms and practices of organizations around the world. As the workplace becomes more diverse and more global in nature, our objective is to help companies change and implement new policies, practices, and cultures that must change as well.

With those expectations as well as the comparable values of equitable treatment, empathy, and decency, comes a comparable axiom that is a burden shared by all of the company's stakeholders, and not just leadership, and that is shared responsibilities, accountability, ownership, and hard work. With new levels of collaboration and cooperation between leaders and employees come new levels of responsibilities of employees to share.

Today, the challenges are not about coerced acceptance or compliance with laws or policies but about recognizing the talent inherent in that more diverse workforce, and how to attract and retain that talent. There is a wider range of diversity and hence talent in that workforce. There is increased competition in the marketplace, thus making it more challenging to attract talented workers. Then, there is the challenge of empowering employees without crossing the fine line of entitlement, and instilling confidence without appearing arrogant. Ultimately, we want to help employees unleash their inner strength—that inner "goddess of go-getting" that lies inside each of us.

# CHAPTER 8

# Unleashing Your Inner Goddess of Go-Getting: the Power of Confidence

*"Feel the beat, look up, and let the music tell the story."*
*– Bhabani Kakati*

Those were the words of advice my mother used to impart when I was about to perform a classical Indian dance piece on stage. You see, I started performing solo dance performances in front of large audiences from the tender age of four. I was classically trained in both the Carnatic dance form of Bharata Natyam, and the Assamese dance form of Xattriya, and was quite in my element being up on stage. Many of my friends who have seen me on stage in different capacities over the years, whether it was as a classical dancer, school performance during house dance or house music, public speaker, debate team member, master of ceremonies, or international keynote speaker, have seen the confidence and stage presence that years of drills and training have provided me with. However, what most people don't realize is that when I was about thirteen years old—so after almost a decade's worth of stage experience—I developed stage fright.

There have been several studies that show that girls lose confidence between the ages of nine and fourteen, which ties into when they go through puberty. An article in *The Atlantic*,[42] "How Puberty Kills Girls' Confidence," accounts for this transition to reasons such as an adversity to risk taking, fear of failure, and perfectionism, but also physical attributes such as a changing body, which also manifests in more defensive body language such as slouching or arm crossing that are often seen in tween and teenaged girls.

The girls surveyed were between the ages of eight to fourteen, and there was an average decrease of thirty percent in confidence levels when the girls rated themselves. Interestingly, until the age of twelve, there was virtually no difference in confidence between boys and girls, but during the key puberty years the average girl was far less confident than the average boy by the age of fourteen.

## Adolescence and fear

For me, this came at thirteen, when I suddenly developed a fear for "What if I forget what comes next?" I never actually did forget my dance routines ever, though. Through hours of practice, and timeless stage rehearsals, the fear became unwarranted, almost like a passing whim of distraction. I was also afraid to make direct eye contact with anyone in the audience in case I was to go wrong, so my mother taught me a nifty trick of looking a few inches above people's heads, which served two purposes; the audience still felt as though I was communicating with them directly through dance, and as I couldn't see individual faces due to the stage lighting, I wouldn't have to worry about any undue reactions! Smart advice indeed, as decades later I use this same very trick during my keynote talks or boardroom pitches!

Ultimately, what got me through this nerve-wracking situation was the discipline and regularity from my dance classes and performances. Dance is after all an art form, a type of meditation, resilience, physical discipline, and love—a love of the music, rhythm, self-expression, and focus. Once I started dancing, I would soon become immersed in the music, and then nothing would get in my way.

At that moment I was in my element, I was unstoppable, I felt empowered.

Fast forward to different life situations, whether I was presenting at a business meeting in finance, or in the final round of a multimillion-dollar pitch for a clinical trials deal, I felt confident, well-put together, prepared, and ready to conquer. That is empowerment.

## Roadblocks to confidence

In reality, however, we all go through moments of self-doubt regardless of your company rank, experience, level of seniority, or celebrity status.

Have you ever stated a fact with a questioning tone of voice? Or have you had defensive body language? Perhaps you have experienced "Impostor Syndrome"? Or used a long-winded explanation to describe something simple?

As a girl growing up in a South Asian home, you are often told to be a good girl and be a good hostess for guests, whereas there isn't the same expectation for boys. Thankfully, this was the perk of growing up in a matriarchal Assamese household where my mother and father equally expected the same household tasks and house chores from both my brother and me. But we saw it at other Indian friend's homes, where girls would sometimes be berated for not being a people pleaser and dropping everything for a guest. What this translates to over time is the girl questioning her worth from a young age, and by continually putting others' needs above hers, not prioritizing or believing in herself. She does not know her worth, and this needs to change.

Whether due to memories or experiences, striving for goals without any clear structure, or not feeling supported by your peers or community, all can lead to the brewing of underlying fears. This could be a fear of failure, rejection, or even uncertainty about the future; the list goes on. Ultimately, it is our own attitudes to facing these fears that hold us back.

- Internal Glass Ceiling – This is an example of a self-imposed barrier for your progression. It is when you strive for a goal but is not a true reflection of your ability or potential.

- Impostor Syndrome – we have all experienced varying degrees of this. Although there has been more research conducted on women, this does not discriminate by gender or background, but affects us all. You could be the CEO of a large conglomerate, an A-list Hollywood actor, Broadway performer, or aspiring soliloquist, and this still affects you. However, what sets these folks apart is their ability to channel fears and doubt into success strategies. For example, if there's a networking gathering, extroverts will be the first in the room, while introverts will need to be invited into the room. If I meet someone extremely confident, the fact that they are so positive draws me into their story. I can turn fear around by going over and complimenting them. I always ask myself how the situation can be a growth opportunity.

- Queen Bee Syndrome – #womensupportingwomen is a popular hashtag, regularly seen as trending on social media. However, the reality is that women don't always support each other, instead sharp elbowing each other, not holding doors open, or openly not extending a helping hand up the career ladder. This I like to term as "Queen Bee Syndrome," a term that is used often in nature, and used to describe a beehive, where there is only one Queen Bee. I have years of personal examples too, where other successful women have ghosted or "unfriended" me as my business and career trajectory took off. Now that we know this phenomenon is actually biological, we can better see why some women appear to show support, so as long as it doesn't seem to step on their toes. Some ways to counteract this are to act on your unique offerings, using your personal stories to excel your passion forward. Working smarter, not harder, allowing synergies to be explored, and responding to other women who are at the same or close seniority to you are all starting points.

- Mansplaining – This is a term women use to describe a scenario where they have given a presentation or response in a meeting, and then a male colleague will paraphrase that same idea and get the credit for it. Rather than get disheartened, I say embrace this! This is a time to take ownership, problem solve rather than feel disheartened or victimized. If you are leading a meeting and want innovative ideas, are you more likely to remember quick punchy responses, or the longwinded granular details? And if you have given a concise response, then no one can then come in and paraphrase what you have said! An exercise in concise communications is to practice a "less is more"–styled ten- or fifteen-second elevator pitch responses daily to help you come straight to the point—and to only go into the detail if pushed to do so later. This same tactic can be employed for negotiating salary raises and pitching to "seal the deal" rather than leave a lingering question.

These are some examples of changing your own perspective and outlook and become inspired for professional and personal success. Rather than venture into a spiral of self-pity and feeling like a victim, let's problem solve instead, rise above and use our empathy skills to think from the other person's shoes and see "why" they think what they think in order to practice and develop winning strategies to success.

Be empowered, not entitled. And don't become a victim to your own fears. With this mindset and resilience, your confidence will prevail as will your ability to communicate and negotiate in order to excel as a future leader.

## Overcoming fears

Using your mind and body to channel emotions of self-doubt into feelings of excitement and readiness can overhaul a negative experience.

Dancing and music have always provided that release for me, such that if I close my eyes then I can relive the happy moment from those memories. One such memory that I will cherish forever is dancing to salsa beats in Guatemala back in the early 2000s straight after I graduated with my fellow backpacking buddies. One summer evening in Antigua, the capital of Guatemala, after a bout of heavy rainfall ended, my friends and I went to the local salsa bar after watching a homegrown Guatemalan pelicula (movie). We were all dancing, and the power of the music was so strong, that minutes later when there was a "templora" or earthquake that evening, which rocked the floor quite literally, the music allowed for a more relaxed and focused mind, so rather than panic, we went straight into problem-solving, earthquake-drill mode.

Having such go-to routines are not only liberating and can help in times of need, but they can do wonders on your own self-confidence.

**Find your tribe**

When I first moved to New York from the UK, I became homesick. So much so that I would gravitate toward any English accent I would hear or watch Wills and Kate's Royal Wedding on repeat just because it made me feel closer to home. What I didn't have in place was a support system. Sure, there was my husband, his friends, and my work colleagues, but without my inner circle of close friends and immediate family, I felt displaced, and I had no idea how hard that would be for me.

As a culture, South Asian women are not taught to raise our hands and show vulnerability, so we don't always know how to ask for help. Instead, there is an expectation to bottle it all up and just deal with life.

It wasn't until I had my son Raahi that I started to feel like New York was home. When he was just a baby, I met new friends, and we shared the bond of motherhood. It was a bond so strong, akin to that of sisterhood. Opening up to each other, and just simply reaching out, enabled us to not only ask for help, but become more open and collaborative. Finding a support network or tribe, is so important.

On the same note, choose your friends and colleagues wisely, as there will be times when you will be faced with negativity. Be prepared to close that chapter and move on. It's one thing to accept constructive feedback, but it's high time to step away when someone constantly brings you down.

## If you can see it, you can be it...

Based on the philosophy that in order to strive to be the best, it helps if you can picture a role model that has traveled on a similar path. So, an exercise I like to give students is the task of visualizing successful role models, who could be anyone from family, friends, peers, mentors, career champions or bosses, to celebrities and well-known personalities, and then jot down traits that stand out. These lists, as can be imagined, are quite varied, as are the role models and often comprise words that describe someone who commands respect, is captivating, an expert in their field, successful, appears confident yet relaxed, has a fighting spirit, possesses grit and resilience, and appears calm under pressure. Ultimately, what bonds all these role models together, no matter which part of the world they are from, is that they all have their own personalities, backgrounds, and journeys in life; they are all unique.

As an example, if two people were to read out the exact same speech, give the same presentation to an audience or pitch to a board, both versions would be different. Tone of voice, body language, recounting stories, personal examples, and presentation style are some examples of such differences.

Quite often we spend far too much time making comparisons to other people's lives, rather than focus on bettering our own. The topic of self-confidence transcends gender, race, and identity. Have you ever thought that an introvert may feel inferior to an extrovert? Or a shorter person to a taller person or someone of slim build to someone of larger frame? Or an overweight individual to someone more in shape?

Ultimately, we are all unique, with our own likes, dislikes, interpretations of the world, and so forth. Even if you are following in the footsteps of others before you, the journey and experiences down the path you have chosen are unique to you. So go forth unafraid and take pride in who you are.

**Channel your inner voice**

Regardless of gender, race, or seniority at work, whether as a seasoned professional or new joiner, homing in on that key ingredient that gives that fighting spirit and confidence to speak up and perform at your best is key. Think of your inner voice as being your soul, your conscience, and ultimately defines who you are.

Some tips for activating your inner voice:

1.  Take the time to pause. Create space for your inner voice to come through. It can be in the form of meditation, a walk in the park, or even sketching in a notebook. Really anything that works for you to unwind and release your mind.

2.  Acknowledge your emotions. Your inner voice need not be an actual word or spoken voice but could just be your thoughts or emotions. It might just be a feeling. So next time your emotions bubble up, don't brush them aside, but embrace them head on and analyze why your thoughts or body is reacting a certain way.

3.  Don't ignore your gut instinct. We've all had that feeling, when you are about to do something or make a decision and when you get that feeling that "something just doesn't feel right." Your gut instinct is a form of your inner voice and may actually be what you need right now.

Ultimately, your inner voice comes from within, and is a combination of your strength and fighting spirit.

It is a part of your empowerment journey, and part of building up your confidence.

**Boost your confidence, free your mind...**

When others feel good, you do too, because confidence is contagious! After all, it's the small things that count, and can be as simple as a smile or hello to a passerby. Have you ever noticed that when you smile at others, open a door for someone, or simply ask someone genuinely how they are, not only do you feel better, but your confidence can have an immediately positive effect on the other person? Simple acts of kindness such as these can brighten up someone's day and show others you care.

Taking the time to listen to others, digest any feedback and acknowledge what they have said, ask meaningful questions in return, and sharing experiences are all acts of kindness and proponents of confidence. Although we cannot control life's situations, we can control our reactions.

I like to think of confidence as a muscle: the more you exercise it, the stronger it becomes. It's similar to walking for the first time as a baby or riding a bike. It takes practice, poise, lots of patience, and a winning spirit as you repeatedly fall down and get back up again, in order to develop muscle memory. Similarly, your confidence can be strengthened with regular practice, just like a muscle.

So just how do you get started to transform into the epitome of self-assurance and poise to meet any challenge head-on?

How confident you appear comes across with what I like to describe as the four P's, namely preparation, perception, power poses, and the key to gelling all the other P's together: practice!

## Preparation

Start by creating your confidence mantra. A mantra is something that becomes part of your daily life, and we want to exercise the confidence muscle, such that it too, becomes part of our everyday routine. Creating a confidence mantra starts by making a self-affirmation checklist, and then including achievements that make you proud, listing your unique strengths, and how you would like others—such as a child, partner, friend, or peer—to see you. You would then post this list everywhere—your computer, refrigerator, mirror—as a daily reminder of your assets and accomplishments. Next, you would write down some positive words to serve as your confidence mantra. As an example, if your words are "unique," "strong," or "I've got this!" you will start your day taking deep breaths and repeating those words five times, "I am unique. I am strong. I've got this!" Practice saying this every morning. Repetition is important for muscle memory, as you want to train your head and mind. The repetition actually helps you believe the words more and more so that your daily mantra becomes a part of you.

It is important to note that your mantra is unique to you. If music, exercise, or yoga serves as an empowering platform for you rather than writing affirmative notes, then use any of those as the basis for your mantra. Think of a boxing match and the contestants as they are led up to the rink. They are wearing their headphones, enacting their confidence mantras as they mentally zone into their winning mind frame. As long as you can repeat the affirmative words with conviction it doesn't matter which avenue you take.

Next, you want to make sure you do your research and know your stuff! Whether you have a board room presentation, dance performance, sports tryout, or job interview, if you don't research what you are doing, if you don't prepare thoroughly, including how to react to difficult or unforeseen circumstances, then if you end up forgetting your lines, or your chain of thought mid-sentence, and have not prepared for that outcome, then your confidence could likely take a hit. Preparation is key to bringing out your best self. Take the playground analogy. By the time of showtime, you want to have fallen so many times, that by now, getting up is a drill that you can metaphorically do even in your sleep.

**Perception**

Research shows that it can take only seven seconds[43] for someone to form an opinion about you, and so you want to make it count! After all, regardless of how you actually are, it is how you are *perceived* to be that becomes the reality.

Having been in so many boardrooms, pitches, and presentations over the last twenty-five years, there comes a time when the "aha" moment of why and when you succeed resonates.

In my pharmaceutical days, I was often the only woman in the room, a young, pretty one at that, and usually by far the youngest too. Regardless of how prepared I was, when I first stepped foot in the room, the rest of the attendees had already formed an opinion about me within the first few seconds of seeing me, whether I had spoken or not. This opinion once formed, stuck in their minds, and was hard to shift.

I knew this was a potential barrier.

However, hailing from the trading floor, and now with years of experience converting skepticism to acceptance and respect under my belt, I had developed a knack of reading the room, and putting my point across with clarity, concision, and conviction. I also knew that people's minds can be changed when you switch the attention to the content. It is quality over quantity, after all.

Some might say slide decks are just fluff, more for decorative purposes, with a "less is more" approach of somewhat sparse but eye-catching content. After all, I wanted to draw the audience toward my words, using the art of storytelling and making eye contact while speaking to or hearing from others.

I would take the time to know my audience in advance and think about what would truly impact them. I spent years exposed to changing social cues and learned quickly how to read the room in various business meetings or cultural settings around the world. Similar to preparing for a TED talk, I took the time to do my homework and research into what the audience would actually benefit from. Given most people fall into the category of being creatures of habit and fearful of change, I knew that ultimately, my audience would not remember the contents of my presentation, but rather two things: 1) how it made them feel, and 2) what was in it for them.

To detract from me to the content of what I was delivering, I would do my homework ahead of time, making sure to know the latest trends inside out. I would quote research backed with peer-reviewed data, provide numbers and create a vision for the company's future. In essence, I painted a virtual picture of how using my solutions could directly impact the company's bottom line, improve their reputation and be their best strategic move possible. My words and style told the story of how I was perfectly equipped to deliver their solution, to a problem the company didn't even know they had, which was far more powerful than the alternative of reading off a non-heartfelt PowerPoint script or resort to trash talking other companies.

Body language, tone, pace of delivery, and pitch of voice, and knowing just when to pause or emphasize certain words were key. I always made sure to dress the part too in order to look and feel my best. Taking note of company attire, I would turn that up a notch, and "become" the goddess of go-getting, repeating my confidence mantras with a resounding "You *got* this!" in my head. Using passion and grit to drive me, I would walk in the room reeking with thought leadership, poise, presence, and confidence.

When sitting in strategic board or executive client meetings, although the topic of diversity and inclusion is on the tips of so many people's tongues, seldom is appearance discussed as a possible area of inclusion and belonging. Interestingly, research shows that good-looking students perform better[44] in tests by as much as one standard deviation, than those less good looking. Similarly, research also shows that overweight or otherwise diverse individuals by appearance face more negative stereotypes[45] than those who are seemingly in shape, dress well, and blend both appearance and personality with their environmental peer group. While this research can be interpreted in many ways, including for many wider implications toward human behavior, bias, value systems, and overall wellness and mental health, what this does tell us, is that when you feel good and have made an effort to dress up or comb your hair a certain way, or stand tall, you feel more confident.

**Power Poses**

Now that I was ready to enter the meeting room, I would take a few deep breaths and strike a "Wonder Woman" power pose either standing or sitting tall, by putting my hands on my hips. Holding a power pose such as this one is an instant way to feel powerful! According to research by Dr. Amy Cuddy,[46] enacting such a power pose for just two minutes, can change your body chemistry from feeling nervous and tense, to becoming more positive (with increased testosterone) and more confident (with decreased cortisol).

Similarly, the reverse is true. For example, if you sit in preparation for your meeting or interview in a slumped position, with your arms crossed, your body chemistry can show decreased testosterone and increased cortisol levels, leading to more apprehension, fear, and tension. Besides, if you are sitting curled up, you may not feel as ready or inclined to contribute to an active team discussion or brainstorming session.

## Practice

This is truly the thread that binds the other three P's altogether: preparation, perception, and power poses. After all, practice makes perfect, as the expression goes. You will want to practice walking and sitting in your outfit, as well as the delivery of your introduction and any ice-breaker jokes or comments, the main presentation, and closing remarks. You can do this with a friend in person or virtually, in front of a mirror and even record yourself on a tablet or smartphone. You'd be surprised at the observations you have of your pitch, body language, and use of filler words such as "um" and "you know."

In fact, you will want to practice so much, that you actually become the role you are preaching. Rather than use the phrase, "fake it 'til you make it," try instead, "fake it 'til you become it." Though we often seek recognition from the outside, true confidence comes from within, right from your core. Your confidence is your voice, your strength, your fighting spirit. Acknowledging factors that shake your confidence such as past experiences, fear of failure or rejection, and your own attitude is key. Confidence can be rebuilt with regular practice and by leveraging a strong support group, such as family, friends, and peers that offers encouraging words. You need someone in your corner who believes in you.

Being passionate about your work comes across as confidence. People who exude passion also exude confidence. Connecting with your passion and choosing your support circle wisely can make a difference. If you spend time with a positive person, it rubs off, and similarly, if you spend time with someone who is constantly grumpy, that rubs off too.

Feeling confident is all about letting your own unique personality blossom, feeling proud of who you are, and having the patience, determination, and winning mindset to "fake it 'til…you become it!" Truly embrace the philosophies of the goddess of go-getting, and Be Bold. Be You. Be Uma.

# CHAPTER 9

## Changing the Narrative

*"Be the change you want to see in the world."*
*– Mahatma Gandhi*

It was a summer weekend in 2002, during the midst of a property transaction I was closing in Marbella, south of Spain. As an early birthday gift to my brother, Rishi, I flew him out to Marbella for the weekend too. I had a keen appetite for investing in overseas real estate portfolios. Realizing property gains and losses, while simultaneously trading and hedging cross-currencies was super exciting to a young trader, now in my early 20s. The plan for the weekend was to get a prescheduled meeting with my real estate lawyer out of the way so that my brother and I could go and celebrate for the rest of the weekend. For one reason or another, my lawyer and I hadn't connected in person yet, so this was also going to serve as the first official meeting too.

When we got to the lawyer's office, he greeted us both, and then proceeded to only look at my brother when responding to questions I had posed. I still remember the look on my brother's face, when a total stranger was talking to him about something he knew nothing about! He kept responding, "You'll have to ask my sister," but didn't seem to get anywhere.

Up until this point, I had only attended my property meetings solo, no matter where in the world the meeting was, and so was rather put off by this rather obvious gender-biased gesture. However, I was in Marbella only for a short while and needed to strike a deal in order to move on. I didn't have the time nor the patience to dilly-dally with who looked at whom and for what. There were two things I needed from this meeting: to close on my property and to make sure I had a lawyer I could trust, especially as I wasn't planning on staying in Marbella full time (stories of corrupt dealings and bribery were aplenty).

Similarly, I thought, "What is the lawyer looking to get out of this?" Foremost, a client that would pay his firm's fees on time, and secondly, to feel confident and trusted enough to represent his clients' Spanish holdings. With that in mind, I posed a confirmation question on his fees, and then proceeded with the same question as before, but this time in Spanish, rather than in English. I went from my first language and his second to my fourth and his first. The immediate impact of that seemingly small gesture from my part was a stark increase in the level of trust. Boom. Mission accomplished.

## If perception is reality, then make it count

Although research shows it takes only seven seconds[47] to form an opinion about someone after meeting them for the first time, it also takes only one tenth of a second[48] to form an impression about a singular aspect, for example someone's face, appearance, or accent, and once made, is hard to shift. So given these constraints, let us shape that first impression as much as possible. For example, a friendly versus firm handshake, eye contact with a smile, attire that dresses the part, and rehearsing personal stories and elevator pitches all fall into this category.

After all, perception, however accurate, is reality. So make sure to prepare for the reality you wish to present at showtime if you're about to go in for a job interview or pitch.

People will judge you on your appearance long before they judge your words or actions, and this judgment has been made only after a tenth of a second. So, make sure to be well groomed and dressed according to the environment and occasion, then turn it up a subtle notch. After all, our minds are continually building a picture, a judgment based on a millisecond guess, stemming from a combination of our own imaginations or past experiences. Having your hair styled a certain way, or wearing a certain suit jacket or heels, can lead people to perceive you as more influential.

Similarly, greeting your audience with a smile with eye contact can make you appear more trustworthy and approachable. So, do offer a genuine smile in those first seven seconds of meeting someone to form a stronger first impression and connection.

Next, it's worth remembering the concept of "less is more," especially for a first meeting. Taking a deep breath and then speak with a clear and concise tone that isn't rushed is key. Conveying too much detail and as quickly as possible can be quite overwhelming and unmemorable. Speaking more slowly and clearly will allow the listener to absorb and digest the information and make you seem more articulate and intelligent. Speaking slowly and with conviction is also a sign of confidence and is at the center of creating a brilliant first impression.

And don't forget your posture and the power poses! Shoulders back, with your chest open and head held high, will not only help you project your voice more clearly, but you will feel more relaxed and appear confident to your audience, thereby strengthening your first impression.

**If perception is reality, then change your reality...**
But what if you blew your first impression? I think we have all had moments like this. But remember, if perception is reality, then you can work to change that perception in order to redefine your reality.

I still remember visiting Basel, Switzerland, and waiting to meet the Global Therapeutic Head of Translational Medicine at Roche during my CNS drug development days. I helped myself to an espresso in the waiting area, hadn't realized there was a gentleman standing directly behind me, and then proceeded to spill the entire espresso shot onto his very well-tailored suit and shoes. I apologized profusely then went on to take a few deep breaths to refocus myself before my meeting where I would be pitching on behalf of my company. As I looked up to enter the boardroom, I was greeted by the same gentleman, who now had coffee stains on his crisp white shirt. He was the global head, that I had flown all these miles to meet. Oh dear.

Having grown up in a family that learned to diffuse a tense situation with a joke, that's what I did. When I introduced myself to the room, I said, "I am Rita, the global head of business development and I am probably the clumsiest person you will ever meet..." The rolling laughter that ensued not only helped diffuse the tension but helped me regroup my own thoughts and drive the perception that I (and therefore my company) was not only punctual and professional, but flexible, good humored, with plenty of charm and charisma. Acknowledging the elephant in the room upfront showed honesty, ownership, and trustworthiness. We won the bid, and over a decade later, my claim to fame, so to speak, is still that espresso-spilling incident.

Many pitches, interviews, and boardroom encounters later, there are two things I have found that ultimately determines the success of your meeting. First, addressing the issue that the decision maker *actually* cares about, and second delivering your pitch as clearly, concisely, and confidently as possible. In order to make all this happen though, walking into the boardroom unprepared won't cut it. Even if you know your materials inside out, take the time to deeply research whatever you can on the team, the decision maker, and what the company needs. This way any anecdotes and examples you give are curated to the actual company and problem at stake. Things to think about are whether this is just a short term "stick on the Band-Aid" type solution to an existing need, or a longer term "nip it in the bud" type of solution, built on a foundation of trust, reliability, and quality, which ultimately would better the company's bottom line. Again, do make sure to ensure your delivery is well rehearsed so that it comes off as concise, charismatic, and as natural as possible.

## Take the bull by its horns

By planning out a well-thought-out roadmap and taking the reins early on, you are setting the tone for the meeting with your presence while also demonstrating your authority and thought leadership in order to steer the ship according to your narrative.

One of the executive women in my leadership coaching cohorts mentioned that she felt quite apprehensive presenting at senior leadership meetings, because once she pitched an idea, a male colleague would almost always paraphrase what she had just said, and in effect be given credit for her hard work. "How do I stop the mansplaining?" she asks. "How do I stay positive after always getting knocked down in meetings?"

## Keep your narrative concise

My response was that it depends on how you think of it. It can be quite powerful from a negotiations standpoint to be able to plant the seed and have the decision-maker finish the sentence for you so to speak, so then you would be the person to help enact *their* vision. That in a way is a win-win, as it leaves them feeling in control, whereas you managed to enact your point, without appearing forceful about it. However, from a communications standpoint, a rule of thumb is to never handover the mic until your point is made, allowing no room for your presence and delivery to be challenged. In the case of my client, she wasn't looking to get a pay raise or steer a hostage situation of any sort, but merely trying to get acknowledged for the work she had been doing.

Rather than sit back and gloat, I asked her to reflect. Why did she lose the mic so to speak? And why was this not a one-off occurrence?

When I used to sit on the receiving end of business pitches, or lead large team meetings, time was short with resources often limited. Therefore, unless an idea could be communicated shortly and sweetly, it wasn't obvious what its relevance was. The most memorable ideas were ones I felt my teams could resonate with and delivered in less than thirty seconds. This is akin to an elevator pitch, and we have all heard that before going to a networking event, take the time to prepare and rehearse your elevator pitch, which could be anywhere between fifteen to thirty seconds long. The same is true for presenting at meetings.

My client confessed to giving her idea as a lengthy presentation, either with slides or verbally, without hitting the punchline and not always making it clear what benefit her idea would bring to the table. If she instead presented her idea as a clear and concise one-liner, then there would be no reason for anyone male or female to then paraphrase what she said.

## Learn from your experiences

I still remember presenting my first-ever moment of discussing trading ideas—the morning rap—at a 6:30 A.M. huddle during the first week of my internship on the equities trading floor of Goldman Sachs in London. When I walked into the room, everyone was talking, and although they initially quieted when I was about to speak, promptly resumed their conversation throughout my "rap." I had no idea how to command the room, and thirty seconds later the hoot was pulled away from me and desks were back to strategizing their own ideas again.

The next week I was up again. I had spent the seven days prior observing how others gave the rap. They just did it. They took the hoot, didn't wait for anyone's permission to start, but just spoke. They spoke in bullet points, not sentences, only presented three ideas, sometimes a fourth after the recap was given, and kept an even tone of voice, pausing at times and emphasizing the buy, sell or hold of each name.

Okay, I was going to crush it, I repeated to myself. I observed, practiced, and did so in front of my buddy, boss and other colleagues.

I practiced until I felt I got it right. In a way it didn't matter what I said, but the delivery was key.

At 5:30 A.M. I was in the office for round two, and then a colleague asked me to get a round of Starbucks for everyone on my desk before I could even sit down. I was in my trainers with my work attire (my go to work-home footwear), and I was going to change into a pair of heels or pumps I kept under my desk. I went to get the coffees, meaning I couldn't read the news like everyone else. This was 2000, so before the days of iPhones, Twitter, and news apps. I couldn't even take my *Financial Times* with me to Starbucks, as I had to somehow balance twelve cups and get through the revolving doors to get back into my building.

It was 6:15 A.M. by the time the coffees were ready, and 6:23 A.M. by the time I was back on the floor, and 6:28 A.M. by the time I gave out all the coffees, as I was still learning names and where everyone sat. I didn't have time to change out of my trainers, and I had not prepared my three ideas for the morning rap. I did however manage to glance at the back page of the FT from another Starbucks customer. On the way to the room, I asked a fellow intern who was always the first to raise their hands in our training meetings, to share their three stock picks for the day. They gladly obliged, and those were the ideas I pitched.

6.30 A.M. and as I grab the hoot, another team manager looks down at my feet, and commented on my trainers. I didn't have time to, nor allow myself to become a victim to the banter. Quick to respond, I commented back on their choice of jeans and that I hadn't realized it was a Friday (it was more customary to wear jeans on the floor on a Friday). Before the laughter fully stopped, I started my rap. I recapped the nights activities and pitched the three ideas even keel, with conviction, as confidently as I could. Done. No interruptions, and I was given a pat on the back afterwards.

It's due to years of practice being subject to last-minute changes and stressful situations, that such "pressure," as some people might feel it to be, doesn't faze me. After all, what's the worst thing that could happen? Work back from there and you will be fine.

## Set the gender narrative

When we think of gender equality, it can at times be hard to differentiate between culturally accepted norms, our own prejudices, and being treated equally. For example, in certain households, it is an untold rule that women will hang around the kitchen and prepare and clean up the food, whereas the men will hang out in the living area and enjoy chatter and conversation with his friends. When it comes to the barbeque however, it is usually the men that will migrate to the outdoors world of preparing grills and meats, again with the women usually left to clean up. These are seen as societal norms, and generally not questioned, but if this type of gender stereotyping does bother you, how would you deal with it?

Part of the answer to this question is generational. More and more these days, particularly in the West, and increasingly in the East too, women and men both perform cooking, caregiving and household activities, although women are still seen to do the lion's share of the household labor. Growing up in my household in London, both my brother and I had to help in the prep and clean up at mealtimes. Similarly, my spouse and I will both take turns in household tasks equally, depending on our schedules. During pandemic work from home times, it would be split by who has a meeting or not, rather than ever have a hint of what my friends often report, "Whose work is more important?" We similarly pass along this messaging to our own children now.

Part of the barriers to sharing these family responsibilities equally is the lack of support from both the workplace and schools. For example, during the pandemic a lot of schools didn't have afterschool activities, and as some caregivers were still feeling uncomfortable about coming into our home, we had to balance and take turns in pick up duties, while simultaneously conducting meetings and our daily work roles.

How did we decide who was going to do what?

We have a joint family calendar and make sure to mark meetings on it. We sit down to discuss the schedule once a week and to confirm who is going to do what. Having the conversation upfront and regularly not only helps you split the responsibility more fairly, it allows you to take ownership. This is sometimes called the "Kitchen Table" principle, where parents would sit down at the kitchen table to plan out the next day, hence forming a parental partnership whereby both parents can decide who will drop off and pick up the kids from school, who will take them to soccer practice or piano lessons, and every other aspect of their day, with each day having a different plan, depending on who will be where, or who has a meeting or some other conflict.

**Gender equality: changing the narrative**
This same thought process can be extended to other gender-equality discussions such as equal pay and family leave. However, without including both men and women around such conversations, corporate cultures, societies, and attitudes will not change.

If you were a mom who took time off to raise your children, or a member of the sandwich generation providing care to an aging parent, employers tend to focus more on your résumé "gap," rather than your credentials. There's a stigma attached to the fact you haven't been earning a paid salary, which some potential employers interpret as you've been doing nothing.

As of 2017, women comprise forty-seven percent of the workforce, and over seventy percent of those women are mothers with children under the age eighteen. 44.5% of those also serve as volunteers or active participants in school or related youth-oriented programs (as opposed to thirty-eight percent of men), and forty percent of those working mothers are the primary bread winners in the household.

Unfortunately, many employers have struggled to keep pace with these changes. A narrative remains in some companies that suggests motherhood is not an actual job and that special employee benefits for working mothers is cost-prohibitive. Also, that working mothers cannot be relied on, because if school shuts down, they disappear.

When I reminisce back to my CNS clinical trials and drug development days and having the conversation with my boss about maternity leave, I was of course offered the measly six weeks leave unpaid, but even more shocking to me was having to file for this as "disability leave." Given that I was now branded disabled, did that mean I would now be getting a disabled badge to display on the windscreen of my car and in essence park anywhere I wanted to?

If we accept the belief that working mothers are not as dependable or focused on their jobs as others because of their childcare concerns, think of how you would be viewed as a job applicant if you were a mom who took time off to raise kids or to provide care to an aging parent. Chances are good that instead of seeing your credentials and accomplishments when viewing your résumé, interviewers see the gap in your employment timeline. There is a stigma attached to the fact you were out of work and not earning a salary during that time. Potential employers can draw the conclusion you were doing nothing.

Knowing first hand that motherhood is arguably the hardest job on the planet, it is up to us to reshape that narrative. It should go something like this: When mothers give birth, they learn very quickly to plan, organize, problem-solve, multi-task, and prioritize like never before. There is perhaps no better training ground than motherhood, to teach women the essentials of managing in the workplace.

When a parent leaves the workforce to raise their family, they are not merely sitting around on a career "break." They very much are still working, though perhaps "career transition" would be preferable to calling it a caregiving role.

We also need to change the perception that the "mommy tax" is solely a mother's issue. Instead, it should be perceived as a family tax. Having a child is a decision that you make with your partner, so any decisions leading to a halt in benefits or career progression—in other words the "tax" you pay—also impacts your partner and the rest of your family.

Some food for thought: What if instead thinking of work as being the priority of our day, with family taking a backseat, we would focus instead on wellness and family, with work as the distraction? Think of those times when you may have taken a family vacation and when you came back to work, your mind was still feeling relaxed, where you approach your full inbox and voicemails with more of a carefree attitude rather than a stressed-out one.

Currently being a fulltime mother—a caregiver—is not counted as a job, so it's left off the GDP calculation. Nannies who are paid on the books are included as a paid service, but only a minority of people pay nannies on the books. A third of women do not return to work after having children, and so we are missing out on huge amounts of quantifiable contributions to society.

Another example is when women choose not to return to work due to the cost of childcare, such as a nanny or daycare. I hear most women talk about how much more they would have to earn in post-tax salary to justify returning to work over having someone else raise their child. The cost just isn't worth it. However, this thought process is totally flawed. Having a child is a family decision. Presumably, if you chose to have a child with a partner or spouse, you would have consulted each other at some point when you planned your family? So what is the difference now? The conversation should be taking place jointly as a family. Can your joint income support the cost of childcare? When you propose solutions to new families at work, such as onsite childcare and shared parental leave, this should be your narrative.

Make it OK for dads to take time off. Showcase dads who work remotely or take paternity leave. Get them to talk about it. The more you shift your own mindset to cater for this new norm, the quicker the needle will shift internally, and a change in corporate culture can then follow.

So, how do we help those companies? How do we change the narrative about women in the workplace and working mothers, and in turn, help change corporate policies to reflect those changes?

For starters, practice what you preach: walk the talk and talk the walk makes a huge difference. If executives routinely use words to represent the most that is possible—and utilize the tools those words represent—the constant repetition and trust in that narrative will ripple across an organization, permeating, strengthening, and becoming a permanent part of its culture.

An Uma workshop we conducted in New York City was on normalizing family leave for fathers, which is still seen in certain industries as a taboo leave to take. We planned the event in honor of Father's Day, so in the true spirit of inclusivity invited both fathers and mothers, as well as no-parent women and men from various industries to take part in a fun roleplaying exercise. The aim was to "experience" the reality of family leave, and the consequences and inadvertent stresses on families if not acknowledged and taken. The outcome was so impactful that at the end of the evening each attendee made a pledge to take forth their newfound realizations and communicate it at their respective places of work. Mission accomplished, with the longer-term hope of a domino effect from the grassroots up to change the corporate narrative.

Offering up truly gender equal benefits helps to balance the roles and responsibilities of new parents, making it easier for both mothers and fathers to share parental responsibilities.

Take Finland as an example,[49] where a women-led government has equalized family leave to seven months for each parent. Prime Minister Sanna Marin's new gender-neutral policy has been designed to eliminate gender-based allowances, with parents permitted to transfer sixty-nine days from their own quota to the other parent, with single parents having access to both parents' allowances.

## Setting the race narrative

When I look back at various encounters over the course of my youth, such as the grass eating experience from my elementary school days, I realize, that before that incident, and once the dust had settled, the *mean* child and I were actually friends. I've had many people ask me over the years about how I dealt with such racist friends, and when I look back, I realize that those children were actually not racist. We were friends. Their parents, their value system, their upbringing taught them to see me differently, but as we spent time together during the day, fears became quashed, and we were five-year-old schoolfriends again. It is true, however, that their parents were perhaps racist and didn't like us being friends, but I would still argue this was a taught reaction, rather than an inherent one.

I'll say it again. Racism is taught, not inherent.

At the time of this writing, my five-year-old daughter, in the midst of kindergarten at her Manhattan private girls' school, came home one day and expressed that her favorite Disney character was no longer Elsa from *Frozen*. Her class was doing portraits exploring the differences in skin tone, and cute as this may have been, she came home to tell me that she was different and no longer looked like her ice-powers-role-model, Elsa. In fact, she also said, "Mama, did you know that if I had even more brown in my skin, then I would be even more special?" So, whereas until this point, my daughter and her friends equally shared role models like the blond-haired blue-eyed Elsa or the black-haired, brown-eyed Meera, now she felt she could only relate to the brown skin toned Meera, or Pocahontas, or Moana. My daughter and her friends were now taught to differentiate by color, and somehow were conveyed the message that to be darker is to be more special.

## Equity vs Equality

There's a fine line between inclusion and reverse discrimination. The terms equality and equity though often used interchangeably, differ in important ways. When we use the term *equality*, we typically mean treating everyone the same; fairly by giving everyone access to the same opportunities. The term *equity* typically refers to proportional representation (by ability, race, class, gender, etc.), which—if not implemented correctly—could inadvertently cause segregation rather than bring people together.

For example, picture two schoolchildren standing side by side behind a fence, trying to view a soccer match on the other side. They are the same age, but of differing heights, so the taller child can easily see the match over the fence, but the shorter child cannot. To be equitable, the school provides a stepping stool for the shorter child so that they too can see the race.

One school of thought would be that by being equitable as in this example, we are actually mollycoddling the natural problem-solving instincts of the next generation. For example, in our parent's generation, if someone couldn't see over a fence, they would have stood on a tree trunk, shuffled toward the front, or found another way to see. They would have learned by undergoing the rules of the playground and be more prepared for the real world, more prepared to survive in the job market, and potentially be more self-aware and better equipped to deal with failure later in life.

In this example, by striving for equity you have successfully singled out an issue that was never previously a handicap. For example, to allow women to compete in a men's four-hundred-meter track race, would you start them a third of the way round the track? Sure, they may have a chance of finishing at the same time, but you've just highlighted that they are getting an advantage by virtue of being a woman. They are getting preferential treatment. That's what equity does in some cases. It brings out an issue that wouldn't have been one. It allows the perception of playing victim or a feeling of entitlement. So instead of creating a fair and equal playing field, you have done the opposite. Surely in the case of the race, it would have been better for the athletes' reputations and their morale to either hold a separate race just for women or have the same rules in a unisex race.

Instead, the focus should be on creating equality. By equality we mean treating everyone fairly, with kindness, while acknowledging there are different communication styles, cultural norms, and habits, for people of different backgrounds.

For example, gender equality should be about educating and providing an opportunity for all genders to be treated fairly. Instead, with the nouveau feminism definition, we are seeing female versions of male chauvinists or female misogynists rather than women trying to create a level playing field.

There are many affinity groups these days. Women's networks, minority groups, sexual orientation, to name just a few. To other employees that are not part of a group, they can feel left out. An example was at a recent MBA class I taught on diversity and inclusion at USC Marshall School of Business. A student, who managers employees in a large tech firm mentioned that even though there are mostly men in the firm, they felt left out when they found out about an outing the women's group had planned. The student was also quick to point out that had there even remotely been the suggestion of a similar, men's group, that would have been a lawsuit right there.

What was he as a senior manager to do? His teams look to him for guidance, and yet he didn't know what to tell them, as he too was confused.

He later mentioned the planned outing was a spa day, and as senior leadership could not think of a way to include the men in an intimate women's retreat, they disbanded the women's group completely.

What would I have done, the class asked? This. As the manager who heard complaints, I would have suggested a coffee meeting with the women's network lead. I would have started with a compliment to get my ask. "I love how the women's network has such creative and meaningful ideas for your group!" Then go in with an ask, "In order for me as a male manager to best support both the male and female members of my team, how can we come up with fun activities together?" Now, problem-solve. Offer a solution. You could follow with something like, "I understand a spa day may be quite intimate, but we love the idea, so perhaps I can see if the men have interest in the same outing on a different day? Or perhaps we can arrange a family day together? Or a dads' group, similar to your moms' one?"

What did this just do? It turned a confusing situation into problem-solving, and a solution was met.

Another affinity group example is from the early 2000s when the women's network at the firm I used to work at had the reputation of women getting together to meet for coffee, so there wasn't much attention paid by senior management. However, what the network actually did, was provide a platform for women across the firm to reach out to each other for professional tips, advice, and mentoring. They met in the canteen due to lack of funding. By getting relevant stakeholders involved with a business plan and growth structure, we changed the narrative such that we managed to officially launch the network, get funding for actual events and outreach, and raise the perception of the women's network as an official platform for growth and strategy for a growing population at the firm.

When thinking about perceptions and changing narratives, another tricky area is women's coworking spaces. While I greatly admire them and the empowerment I feel after visiting or presenting at one, I can understand why other women and men see these spaces as actually causing division, so they are arguably the opposite of gender equality. After all, a male-only coworking space in this day and age is a lawsuit waiting to happen, and so moving away from coworking spaces to spaces that are open to all can actually create increasing rifts and barriers to gender equality.

Ultimately, striving for equality can also ensure a fair and equitable solution for all.

**Challenging the norm**
"When in Rome, do as the Romans do" … or should you?

In Chapter 6 we talked about understanding the ways of the playground, an analogy for listening to and reacting to social cues, environmental, and workplace cultural norms. Indeed, no matter where in the world we are, from an early age we have been conditioned to "fit in." And if we don't, then society dictates that any repercussions is solely our fault.

We have been trained to keep our personal lives separate from our professional lives, our views to ourselves, speak only when spoken to, and the list goes on.

Our inner voice, our personality, our thoughts remain as just that—inner.

So how can you bring out that inner voice, unleash your confidence, and allow your personality to shine? After all, this is what makes diversity and inclusion go hand in hand.

If you're a company, your business thrives when your team members contribute alternative ideas that promote innovation. We call this creativity. And diverse voices result in creativity.

However, we have been "taught" and prepared that to succeed in the workforce we must think like everyone else. We should agree with our peers and, it goes without saying, laugh at our boss's jokes.

The term "groupthink" was first used by social psychologist Irving Janis, to describe the psychological phenomenon of a well-intentioned group working together to make decisions, and by doing so, striving for harmony and consensus. The flip side, however, is that groupthink discourages individuals from seemingly disagreeing with others in the group, thereby keeping their ideas and any creative thoughts, to themselves.

In a postgraduate class I recently taught, there were two female students from India, one a recent engineering graduate from Stanford, and the other a senior executive at a Silicon Valley tech company. They both mentioned how much anxiety and pressure they felt about speaking up in meetings. They feared that what they said would be bigger than them, that it would reflect on all women from India. So they chose not to speak up in meetings at all, for fear of "saying something inappropriate."

In this case, both their managers would simply ask if anyone in the team had any thoughts or feedback, and if anyone didn't speak up, the assumption was that they didn't have anything to say, and so the managers would simply move on. I asked them how they would prefer their managers handle the situation differently.

Their feedback was that a manager could approach them privately and say something along the lines of, "Hey, I notice you don't always share your thoughts in our meetings, but I would really love to hear your thoughts on the topic. Is there anything I can do in a meeting to make it easier, or is there another way you'd like to communicate with me that would be less stressful but allow you to contribute?"

Both women said they would have chosen to communicate by email, then by talking to their manager privately.

So how can you move away from the norm, and reinvigorate your creativity, your inner voice at work? Here are some hacks to get you started:

- Bring yourself to work. Yes, there is professional etiquette, but don't let that stop you from shining through. The once upon a time of leaving your personal experiences under lock and key at home has now changed.

- Take time to observe. Spend some time taking in what's what at work, understand current processes. Then think about what stands out to you and what could potentially be changed.

- Remain enthusiastic and helpful in your team meetings and tasks. This way you are seen as a team player, can build rapport with your colleagues, with the aim of having added credibility when presenting your points.

- Take a step back and listen. To formulate your opinions and ideas for change, start by analyzing the current method of doing things. That means be the "fly on the wall" in order to observe, listen and take detailed notes.

- Then say what you think, remembering that:

- Presentation is key. In order to voice your opinions in a constructive way, first acknowledge any positive feedback or observations from the current methodology. Then present your alternative thoughts showing any research or background information you can provide.

- Structure your delivery. Order your key points logically and methodologically, providing alternative discussion points. Leave time for debate and encourage discussion.

- Follow up. If you want to change something, then stick with your idea. This means getting feedback, taking it onboard, then making any necessary adjustments in order to see it through. Be proactive and carve out airspace to follow up on your idea.

**The onus is on everyone**
There is often the thought that women act a certain way just because they are women.

Upbringing, however, plays a huge part when it comes to confidence and how you conduct yourself. For example, how many parents brought up their daughters *exactly* equally to their sons? Were daughters taught to open doors for men just as sons for women? At restaurants why do a majority of men get the check? Sexism is inbred. Same goes for cultural stereotypes. Women are taught to be submissive in certain cultures. These cultures are mixed in around the world whether you are in the United States, the UK, or India as an example.

In Great Britain, according to Ipsos Mori and the Global Institute of Women's Leadership at King's College London,[50] only thirteen percent men agree that a man staying at home to look after his children is less of a man, compared to eighteen percent globally. In India thirty-nine percent of men think it is belittling for them to raise their children and seventy-six percent in South Korea. In the Netherlands it's less that ten percent.

To reiterate from Chapter 7, the onus for changing the narrative isn't just the responsibility of a single entity. The onus is on everyone: corporations, small and mid-sized enterprises, the education system, policy makers, government, lawmaking bodies, and a patriarchy that is particularly prevalent in certain cultural backgrounds. The entire system is responsible, from conversations around the dinner table at home or with friends and coworkers, to policy makers changing terminology and extending flexible benefits to both women and men.

New narratives around gender equality, race and cultural change require thoughtful, disciplined, ongoing commitment to the concept of flexibility. First, people learn to be flexible in their interpretations and perceptions of people and circumstances, then mental flexibility is required to traverse the path from awareness, to action, to accountability. Also, write down your interpretations of traditional definitions of certain words such as diversity, inclusion, openness, flexibility, minority, then offer additional, wider and sometimes challenging definitions.

As businesses grow in size and revenue, so do the investments made to fuel that growth. Technology, real estate, utilities, office equipment, travel expenses and personnel, are all essential expenditures in managing the day-to-day operations of an enterprise.

None are as essential, or as expensive as its employees though, which by far are a company's greatest investment.

Day by day, company by company, country by country, interview by interview, employers are beginning to recognize these blind spots, and we are on a path to eliminating them. Companies are becoming increasingly aware and able to look past those labels that have historically blinded them. We are slowly moving beyond the issues of categories, and labels, and quotas, to that place where we assess and judge applicants for their value and character, as opposed to their resume. We are slowly evolving to a place where companies value decency over pedigree. We are making progress.

But we are not there yet.

**Changing your narrative**

There is a part of our brain known as the reticular activator, which enables messages we receive into our brains to be programmed to be alert when we see or hear those same things. For example, if you are looking to buy a new red dress, at that moment it seems like everyone around you has a red dress, or similarly if you hear a new word for the first time, you hear that same new word in three different conversations during the course of a week.

The reticular activator goes to work almost immediately after we are born, where messages heard as a three-year-old get filed away, forming the earliest versions of our life's narrative. "You're a bright child with a bright future ahead of you" or "Too bad you weren't born a boy, you're really good at fixing things." Whatever those early childhood messages, the reticular activator records them and files them away.

Those messages are the beginnings of our belief systems, which follow us into our youth. Similarly, we hear messages from our teachers, coaches, or others that influence us, such as "You have a good way with words" or "I don't think mathematics is a good subject for you" or "You are very artistic." Those messages are imprinted in our brains and remain with us right up into our college years and beyond.

These beliefs then become our reality. There is a scientific phenomenon known as the Pygmalion effect.[51] Numerous studies have shown that when teachers are told positive things about a student, those students perform better. Other studies have demonstrated that when a manager is told a team member performs well under pressure just before undertaking a high-stress task, their performance goes up by as much as thirty-three percent.

The same process collectively expands to become regional, and sometimes national and multinational narratives, forming the foundation of our cultural and societal beliefs. It is those cultural and societal beliefs that intermingle with company attitudes and practices to formulate corporate narratives. For example, men sitting at the head of the table in home settings, to hearing statements such as "Men make the most effective leaders" in the workplace, or culturally having the norm of respecting your elders and seeing companies promote staff based on seniority rather than competency.

The good thing about the reticular activator is just as it was originally programmed, it can be re-programmed. Whatever beliefs found their way into our minds, from childhood, or a current or recent boss, can be changed.

Yale University undertook a study to explore the secrets of a long life.[52] They followed adults for twenty years, closely monitoring their diets, exercise habits, and many other of the obvious health-related variables, and their mental attitudes. Attitude was the most significant factor, where people who had a positive view of aging in midlife lived an average of 7.6 years longer than those who had a negative view. In other words, if you say, "I think getting older is going to rock," you're likely to live 7.6 years longer than your friend who says, "I think getting older is going to suck."

Changing our narrative therefore begins by changing belief systems. By reprogramming our own reticular activator, we become influential in reprogramming that of others. That is how we go from being outliers to being influencers of policy.

Finding our voice and knowing we have something of value to contribute is the first step. Speaking that voice is the second. It is the subtle, nuanced meaning of our words that shape our narrative, which differ, depending on the global perspectives we bring.

# CHAPTER 10

## Lessons from Around the Globe

*"Those who have a strong sense of love and belonging
have the courage to be imperfect."*
*– Brené Brown*

Diversity and inclusion doesn't mean the same everywhere, so pigeonholing assumptions can actually cause segregation and confusion.

For example, during the atrocious events surrounding the murder of George Floyd in 2020, I was asked to give several talks to various offices of multinational companies. While discussing race, systemic bias, and privilege may have been very relevant to discuss with employees across the United States or the UK, giving the same training or talk to members of an India or other Asian office bore no relevance. Diversity is meant to be representative of your demographic, and relevant to the issues faced in the locality.

To demonstrate, hiring more diverse talent in Russia may mean a focus on how to help colleagues feel integrated when they have joined from a different location such as India. In New York, this may lean toward more of a focus on awareness for allyship and understanding privilege. Similarly, in India, this could mean discussing ways of treating women more equally and extending job opportunities to those from different states and caste backgrounds.

## Ours is a global journey

Being from the UK and now residing in the United States, it could be easy to be lulled into that parochial perspective when thinking about our mission. Fortunately, my speaking engagements take me to other parts of the world, where I realize very quickly, there is more work to be done.

At a recent policy forum at the epicenter of decision-making and impact in Europe—Brussels, I was one of a handful of women chosen from around the world to discuss new ideas to influence corporate change. I was an ambassador of the West, representing the United States and the United Kingdom. The visit included delivering a keynote address at the European House of Parliament on the topic of "How Increasing Women's Influence is Better for the Global Economy."

A major part of that discussion was and is about the need to change the narrative of men's vs. women's roles in society. For example, taking time off work following the birth of a child. Or which parent is normally associated with dealing with a last-minute childcare emergency.

Recognizing the diverse business practices around the world, and the diverse views on women in the workplace, I was very sensitive to those differences. Though norms and business practices vary widely around the world, there is one commonality that every entrepreneur and CEO understands, no matter where they are from: money.

So, I began my speech by painting the picture of an ideal world, where if women were to play an identical role in the labor markets to that of men, then, according to research by consulting firm McKinsey[53], as much as twenty-eight trillion dollars, or twenty-six percent, could be added to the global annual GDP by 2025. However, with there being only relatively fewer women CEOs in Fortune 100 companies, there is an obvious disconnect.

Eighteen percent of men globally feel that staying at home to look after children makes you less of a man.[54] This figure fluctuates depending on the country, symbolizing that a changing mindset isn't merely an issue for corporate culture. Years of cultural traditions embedded into societal norms may also be contributing to the prevention of true gender parity throughout society, whether it's work-based or otherwise.

An official from the European Parliament and I were later chosen as spokespersons to present an action plan gender equality to the other international delegates on one of the official goals of the United Nations Sustainable Development Plan.

First, we presented the importance of understanding that gender equality means that everyone is treated fairly and equally, rather than boosting one gender vs. pushing another down. We then talked about fact-based research, delineating regional, cultural, societal norms and nuances, and the need to avail existing regulations, policies, and legalities. Presenting case studies depicting economic impact would have greater meaning if conveyed jointly by men and women as allies, where roles and responsibilities should be split 50/50.

In order to increase women's influence, we need to prioritize confidence, recognize unconscious bias in the workplace, and companies need to make a real commitment to inclusion rather than checking off the diversity box. I ended with an ask. Each influencer in the room was to pledge action. To hold the hand of a woman in their own place of work and make an actual pledge to extend her the proverbial ladder to climb up.

I am so thankful to the changemaking organizations Women Influence Community, and Diplomatic World for bringing together such a formidable group of highly influential and powerful women from all over the world and allowing me to share my message to this very special sisterhood.

It is forums like these, and similar initiatives around the world, that are the growing thousands of drumbeats that will reshape this narrative about women in the workplace and working mothers around the world.

But what about those other countries around the world?

Well, the bad news is some countries have deeper cultural norms and practices that make our challenge more difficult. The good news is that in virtually every one of those countries, the journey has begun. While some countries and their governments are taking positive actions and making strides to accommodate these changes and others lag behind, all are pursuing the initiative to change the narrative.

Let's look at some of the countries that have proactively made women and minorities a focus via initiatives, cultural progress, and in some cases legal action.

## Singapore
Singapore is one of the more progressive countries in the East. In recognition of more working mothers, the government created a tax initiative called the Working Mother's Child Relief (WMCR) program. The primary objective is to reward families with children and encourage mothers to remain in the workforce.

## Taiwan
Taiwan provides working mothers and their newborns a confinement hotel or a residence where medical staff are on hand around the clock to tend to the needs of new families. Maternity leave for most women has been extended to two months.

## Egypt
Egypt has embarked on the Women and Memory Forum (WMF) that allows women to challenge traditional narratives and redefine their role in society and in the workplace. Since its founding in 1998 the WMF has extended its reach into Palestine and Sudan.

## Japan
Japan has struggled to come to grips with the rising number of women in its workforce and is further challenged by the intensity of its overall work culture. Unequal treatment, harassment, and compensation remain dominant issues for women. The World Economic Forum placed Japan at one hundred and twenty out of one hundred and

fifty-seven[55] countries in terms of gender equality in 2021, driven in large part by a thirty percent gender wage gap. A 2012 harassment lawsuit brought several issues to the fore as has the creation of a variety of women's organizations, including the Women's Action Network, the National Women's Education Center, the Asia-Japan Women's Resource Centre, and the Working Women's Network.

## India

India is both the country of my heritage and the birthplace of my parents. Born and brought up in Assam, India, and raised by traditional Assamese values, my parents immigrated to the UK where I was born and brought up and experienced a very different culture. So, in many respects, I experienced the best of both worlds: the traditional values of my Assamese heritage and the more modern views of Western society.

While mainland India still holds true to its traditional patriarchal views of a woman's place as is in the home, Assam and the northeast continues to lead instead by their matriarchal values. Its strong British influence also helped to open the door to the more "unconventional" notions of women and mothers being a part of the workforce. The country, in many respects, serves as a bridge between the East and the West. As the country's economy has grown, so has its views toward working women. Its society continues to battle an entrenched male-dominated workforce, more and more educated, middle-class women are emerging in the workforce.

And those women have two significant assets that women in other parts of the world don't have: a close-knit family unit, and access to an inexpensive domestic labor workforce. Post-marriage, many women move in with their husband's parents, giving them a family-based support system and resources.

Indian female role models have also aided in changing the narrative about females in the workforce. Naina Lal Kidwai, who retired in 2015 as chairman of HSBC India, and was the first Indian woman to graduate from the Harvard Business School in 1982. She began her banking career when banks not only did not offer flexible hours, but she often had to go to a different floor just to find the women's washrooms.

Role models such as Kidwai and Indra Nooyi, the Indian American business executive and former CEO of PepsiCo, have opened the doors for a new narrative for Indian women everywhere.

Ours, indeed, is a global journey. My speaking engagements have taken me far beyond the United States, the UK, and Continental Europe. I have traveled to, given keynotes at, and advised decision-makers in so many cities from Moscow, Sochi, London, Nottingham, Brussels, Madrid, Paris, New York, Guwahati, Delhi, Kolkata, Mumbai, Shillong, Sirmaur, Los Angeles, San Francisco, Columbus (Ohio), Toronto, Kanya, Zambia, Israel, Melbourne, and many other cities, states and countries around the world to deliver this message. The narrative is different in each. Not only from country to country, but city to city. When I visit other parts of the world, I think to myself of how much more advanced we must be in the west. Then, I speak and conduct workshops in smaller, more remote cities and companies in the United States, and I'm reminded of the same challenges that still remain here, at home.

But we are making strides, even in some of those most remote corners of the globe. We simply journey on, change attitudes, beliefs, narratives, policies, and business practices, one country, one company, one mindset at a time.

# EPILOGUE

## The Tao of Uma

*"To lead people, walk beside them."*
*– Lao Tzu*

"Taoism" is a philosophy that has its roots in eastern Asia and is best known for its teachings of being in harmony with the universe. Not to be confused with any religion, Tao (pronounced Dao), simply means "the way." The Tao of Uma, roughly translated, means "The Ways of Uma."

This book is further testament to these worldly experiences, bringing together personal anecdotes and thought leadership from my various experiences around the world.

As I draw this book to a close, I look back on the lessons and steps that we have covered, and in some cases still need to pave for the journey ahead to a more diverse and genuinely inclusive future that understands, acknowledges, and treats everyone fairly, regardless of their background, gender, cultural or religious beliefs, or political viewpoints.

In Chapter 1 we have seen examples of the many shades and nuances of diversity and the effects of pigeonholing based on preconceived stereotypes from skin tone to regional and culinary differences.

Chapter 2 analyses the manifestations and costs of these many biases that have accompanied anyone who identifies as a minority.

Chapter 3 takes this further by looking at why people leave companies, and the implication on the workforce and companies' bottom lines.

Chapter 4 delves into the importance of understanding and having flexibility, and the evolution and relevance of empathy. We then talk about successful company culture and how it can best be shaped.

Chapter 5 talks about the importance of a top-down leadership approach, one that is dependent on the evolution of IQ and EQ into DQ, the decency quotient.

Chapter 6 looks at culture from the grassroots up, talking about the importance of us all learning and sticking within certain "ways" of the world, similar to how children learn their social interaction basics from picking up the unspoken rules of the playground.

Chapter 7 talks about the "how" of achieving this, by actively being responsible for our own actions and deeds. The thinking being that if we all took ownership, then in theory we would be proactive changemakers helping to shape the world around us.

Chapter 8 talks about confidence and building up our inner strength, with methods to unleash that inner goddess of go-getting that already lives inside all of us.

Chapter 9 acknowledges that although we cannot shape circumstances, we can choose our reaction in order to influence or define what happens next. It is through this ethos that we can become active changemakers.

Chapter 10 ties everything together with examples and anecdotes from around the world.

Through our own journey at Uma, we've had the privilege of meeting and speaking with many cohorts of amazing and accomplished women and minorities who have embraced their heritage and backgrounds, overcome challenges and obstacles, and thrived and achieved thereby setting an example for the next generation of enterprising and aspiring young girls and boys. While many roadblocks still need addressing, we cannot help but be optimistic toward the future as we progress to a society and culture that truly values diversity and inclusion through decency, empathy, mutual understanding, and confidence, and we are grateful and humbled that we can be a small part of bringing about that change.

Here are some pointers to leave you with:

- This is your life, so stop comparing yourself to others

- Carve your path according to your vision, not anyone else's

- Everyone wants to feel like they belong, so take the time to let them know they matter; hear and see them

- Repeat your daily mantras every day

- Believe in yourself and unleash your inner goddess of go-getting!

This book hopes to inspire, build up, and empower others. After all, it is this Tao of Uma that leads you to realize and achieve your goddess of go-getting and to feel empowered. And once you feel empowered, it is then your duty to empower others!

# Words of Inspiration

*"Your power is in your individuality, in being exactly who you are."*
*– Jennifer Lopez*

Beyond our seminars and conferences across the world, we also spread our empowerment message through our Uma team voices, global ambassadors, as well as through The Uma Show, a regular television talk show on Mana TV International that I host, where I am in conversation with accomplished South Asian role models who have broken through the proverbial glass ceiling in some way. Their backgrounds are far and wide, from being a multi award-winning quantum physicist to a former White House official, Oscar winning TV and film producer, Olympic swimmer, Wimbledon tennis player, to luxury designers, vocalists, chefs, entrepreneurs, and noteworthy professionals. Each guest brings their unique perspective on their journey, accomplishments and challenges faced.

Here are some inspirational quotes from recent show guests, as well as Uma team members and ambassadors:

## Quotes from *The Uma Show*

"Something I wish I believed, truly, when I was earlier in my career: 'people over success'." – Kavita Mehra, Executive Director, Sakhi for South Asian Women, NY, USA

"When you communicate, think about the message you want to get across and who your message is going to resonate with. When you write, do it for yourself. Even if no one picks up your piece, it is important to keep your writings for yourself to look back on." – Sejal Sehmi, UK Editor, Brown Girl Magazine, London, UK

"Without dark, there wouldn't be light and without dark there wouldn't be light, so it's like the 'yin' and the 'yang', which helps you appreciate your life and what you have that much more." – Vicky Vyas, Contemporary Artist, Toronto, Canada

"If you can develop a niche, something that you are talented in, and you can develop that every single day, then you can carve your own following and expertise, and the media will come and find you." – Joya Dass, Former news anchor and Founder of Ladydrinks, New York, USA

"As an entrepreneur, chef and multi-restauranteur, you constantly need to be thinking two steps ahead. That means thinking about every position in your business and looking to hire people who can do it better than you." – PriaVanda Chouhan, Owner and Executive Chef, Desi Galli, New York, USA

"Don't be scared of failure. Entrepreneurship is a long marathon, and if you think it's only going to take one, two or three years, no way! Ten to fifteen years is what you need to give it, for you to truly emerge and make that breakthrough, and figure out what you're made of." – Aanchal Bhatia, Founder & CEO of Sydenham Clinic, Houston, USA

"When you go to an event, make the effort to talk to people who are not necessarily in the center of the room. Just as someone once helped bring you into a conversation, pay it forward by helping others." – Sujatha Zafar, Programs Lead for Inclusion and Diversity at IHS Markit, New York, USA

"Be kinder about conversations on topics such as single parenthood or divorce. Be less judgmental, but still do have the conversations, because that's how you build awareness with the hope of changing mindsets over time." – Sonja Thomas, Associate Professor, Gender and Sexuality Studies, Colby College, Maine, USA

"My dad used to say, 'No mistakes in Kumon, and no mistakes on your forehand,' which is the mantra we lived by during our younger years, as my dad believed in strengthening both our bodies and minds." – Neha Uberoi, Former Professional Tennis Player, Co-Founder & CEO of South Asians in Sports, New York, USA

"For decades women have been pitted against each other. Take for example 'Who wore it best,' articles or 'Megan vs. Kate' dress polls. There seems to be a constant need to drive comparison and competition as women. However, if we as women let down our guard a little, allow other women in, treat them as sisters-in-arms and unite, then we have capacity to breakthrough so many barriers." – Rupinder Kaur, Founder of Asian Women MEAN Business, London, UK

"For creative journalism, show your passion, write blogs, volunteer at your local radio station, grow your portfolio. You can film your own video on your phone these days and edit it yourself. Secondly, build your contacts, as this industry is all based around who you know, so keep on connecting with people." – Nina Goswami, Creative Diversity Lead, BBC, London, UK

"Going from Uma's advice, start with 'Be Bold!' Always start with what is possible, and let others tell you why it can't be… Then take risks, take chances. You don't have to know everything. Believe in yourself to be able to learn it. If you have one strong eye and one weak eye, you are only going to develop the weak eye if you cover the strong one. So, if you're really good at something, leverage that, but then start focusing on building the things that you are not so good at, so that you continue to develop yourself and your skillset." – Arpa Garay, President of Global Pharmaceuticals, Commercial Analytics and Digital Marketing, Merck, New Jersey, USA

"At work, make sure you have a great workplace to work at, with both women and men mentors to look up to, as you will pick up so much more. At home, we could all learn how to be better partners and support for each other. Also, get yourself three dogs and a cat, so if you have children, the pets can keep the children entertained!" – Sharmila Rudrappa, Professor of Sociology and Director of the South Asia Institute, University of Texas, Austin, USA

"Following from the words of the late Justice Ruth Bader Ginsburg, 'dissent speaks to a future age,' so if you have an opinion and a voice, it might not be heard today, but it doesn't mean it won't leave an impression on someone who'll carry that message forward. So, use your voice, state your truth and fight for the things that are meaningful to you, and do it in a way that makes people want to heed you." – Sumana Setty, Co-Founder of Commit-2-Change, and Partner at Kirkland and Ellis, New York, USA

"Make your goals your own. There is no right or wrong goal, and if there is something you want to achieve, it's not impossible. Just stick to it. The journey sometimes has its ups and downs, but it's really about enjoying the ride and enjoying the journey. Surround yourself with people that support you and that make you happy. Don't just follow your passion but allow your passion to follow you." – Shikha Tandon, Former Olympian Swimmer, Director of Partnerships at Silicon Valley Exercise Analytics, Silicon Valley, USA

"Define what you want and go after it. Do what you love but have a practical way of staying independent. You need to think about the life you want to have, more than any dream you can create today. If you want to switch your profession, or the one you have is going away, then reinvent yourself. Take courses and keep learning. Finally, don't forget to balance the whole you, and take time off if you need to." – Khadija Mustafa, Senior Director, Head of Global Partner Ecosystem, Autonomous Systems, Technology and Research, Microsoft, New York, USA

"Resilience, passion, and believing in yourself is important. Learn from others, but don't copy others. Try to find your own voice, your own style, and own message. The truer you are with yourself, the more your message will resonate with the world. You are unique, so try to preserve that uniqueness. Work hard, but work smart, so that you can quickly pivot to earning to support yourself, if needed." – Ila Paliwal, Indian Vocalist, Songwriter and Producer, New York, USA

"Be gender blind so that you can truly use your skills to better yourself. Don't think that because you are a woman you cannot become part of a camera crew or be on location. That is your own bias speaking. If you want to do, just do it." – Swati Thiyagarajan, Oscar-winning Conservation Journalist, Author, Filmmaker and Storyteller, South Africa

"Raise your hand for opportunities. Volunteer for roles that remotely interest you. Don't be afraid of going on a new adventure. Take the risk. There is always going to be a combination of hard work and luck, but also count on your social network. Lean on your support network, your tribe and push yourself." – Baishakhi Taylor, Dean of the College and Vice President for Campus Life, Smith College, Massachusetts, USA

"Government, private sector, philanthropists, and regular people are all responsible for shaping the next generation. What happens in the home, taught in the classroom and followed in society matters. The person that has the most power is the mom. A mother is a child's first teacher. What she tells that child about giving dignity to other human beings is something that will go into that child as they grow up." – Farah Pandith, World-leading expert and pioneer in countering violent extremism, Washington DC, USA

"Journeys start from within you. You can't empower anyone else unless you yourself are empowered. Find out what it is that makes you happy, makes you feel content, and makes you feel that your soul is going to sing. Many of us live our lives with a song unsung in us, and we need to change that. Find your calling, even if isn't exactly what you planned, and calm that unrest in you. Only then can you feel empowered, and then you must make it your duty to empower others." – Loya Agarwala, Founder and Managing Partner, UCan Centre, Guwahati, Assam, India

"Be willing to learn. You have got to keep your cars and eyes open and trust your gut instinct. Have that sense of confidence in your own viewpoint, and then be positive, engaged and enjoy the journey. Failure does knock your socks down but learn from it. It's very humbling to fail and is much needed to traverse the messy road to success." – Babi Ahluwalia, Co-Founder and Creative Director of Sachin & Babi, Co-Founder of The Good Kloth Company, New York, USA

"Do what you do from a place of love and bring your full self to work. If you don't come to your work from a place of abundance, it's never going to fulfill you and it's never going to let you get to the next level that you are capable of. Step into those feminine traits that we as women leaders have within us. Countries and organizations that have survived the pandemic, and that were led by female leaders, were led authentically. At no point were they seen as weak, but they exhibited signs of tremendous empathy, collaboration and care." – Mona Sinha, Co-Founder of Raising Change, Founder of the Asian Women's Leadership University, New York, USA

"When your passion drives you and you want to make a difference, the adrenaline comes in and you just get going. It is also important to take time to enjoy the small things in life, which are actually the big things in life, whether that is your family, gardening, cooking, reading, or event traveling, because these are the things that nurture your soul." – Seema Kumar, Global Head, Office of Innovation, Global Health and Scientific Engagement at Johnson & Johnson, and Founder of SEEMA, New Jersey, USA

"Always look up! When you are feeling down, you look up to feel better, but also looking up means to aim high. Even if you don't make it all the way to the top of the mountain, if you aim for the highest mountain, you are probably going to get a pretty good spot and have a great view. Don't compromise on what is important to you and your own principles. Looking up is also about curiosity, so if you're a child who has looked up at the stars and wondered what's out there, then you have already taken the first step toward being a scientist." – Shohini Ghose, Professor of Physics and Computer Science, Wilfred Laurier University, Toronto, Canada

"Hard work never goes to waste. Just work hard, be smart, be clear about what you want, and when you decide what you want, hustle and go fight for it. There is no substitute for hard work. Everything that seems so glamorous with startups, successes, or magazine articles took at least ten years to get there. So when being seduced by the results, don't overlook the hard work." – Oshiya Savur, VP of Marketing, Luxury Brands, Revlon, New York, USA

"Become comfortable with being uncomfortable, because growth comes from being uncomfortable. After all, if you are in your comfort zone, you are not learning. Given we are perfectionists, we need to understand that we are all actually work in progress and will continue to be so until the day we leave this planet. Also, rather than measure ourselves through KPIs, or key performance indicators, we should use instead KJIs, or key journey indicators, as that is indicative of our goals in our career journey." – Vandana Saxena Poria MBE, Serial Entrepreneur, Pune, India

"Don't be afraid of going it alone, as your shadow is always with you. When the sun is on top of your head, your shadow is a reminder that you are you, so don't let anybody talk you down or distract you from your dream. You are the only person who can make your dream come true. And if you don't yet know what your dream is, do what you love. Whatever you want to be is deep within your heart, and you'll find it one day." – Rachna Nath, NASA Solar System Ambassador and STEM Educator, Phoenix, USA

"If there is something you want to do, don't be afraid of failure. Just get out of your comfort zone and just do it! If you never try, you'll never know, so, just do it!" – Chandrabali, Ghose, Founder and CEO of Bioharmony Therapeutics, New York, USA

"Be your own authentic self, rather than spend countless numbers of years seeking endorsements from everyone else, be it your parents, your professors, your colleagues, or whomever. You only have one life to lead, so go on and Be Uma! Be a go-getter and do what you want to do! And then go on to achieve that. And if you don't, it's really not the end of the world, because when you've tried, it's just as good enough. It's not something you have to do for the rest of your life, as you can change your path as many times as you want." – Sharmishta Chatterjee-Banerjee, Policy Director, Internationalisation, at Radboud University's Nijmegen School of Management, The Netherlands

"Believe in yourself and never think that what you have to contribute is unimportant. Don't let self-doubt get in your way and think that only if you say something super smart you will make a difference, because anything that you say is going to help. Then, you have to hustle. You cannot expect someone to invite you to accept this job. No, it doesn't work that way. You have to go for it, you have to push and then you have to get known. You have to work hard, and also make sure people know who you are and that you exist." – Swati Karkun Sen, VP of Strategic Initiatives at NBC News, New York, USA

"Keep moving, keep moving forwards. And even if the acceleration isn't always what you expect given what is going on in your life, always keep making progress, trust the process, and continue to stay connected to your career and your personal development." – Sonal Rinello, Co-Founder and CMO of Hello Career Guru, Connecticut, USA

"Your career path is unlikely to be linear, so be prepared and open for change, because things will change. Then seek out and build a network of mentors and work colleagues that fit your work personality, aptitude, and strengths. It is very hard to sustain something that isn't consistent with who you are." – Romita Shetty, Managing Director, DA Capital, New York, USA

"Learn as much as you can. Talk to people in the field and learn about people in different contexts. Your experiences in life will directly impact the advice and work you do for your clients. The more you work on yourself and heal yourself first, the more enhanced your work with others will be." – Sarika Seth, Clinical Psychologist, Thrive Psychology, Los Angeles, USA

"Think long term. Nothing happens on an immediate basis and there aren't things you can do that pay off right away, but they will eventually. With persistence and consistence, there is the power of compounding that results when with these two things happen, especially when you show up every day and you chip away at the problem." – Sairee Chahal, Founder and CEO, SHEROES, New Delhi, India

"Dream. Dream. Dream. And set your goals. And even if your goals get reset, continue dreaming. Life is like a boxing ring. Defeat is not declared when you fall down. It is only declared when you refuse to get up. So no matter what, just keep rising and shining again!" – Adrija Biswas, Corporate Leader, Innovator, Motivational Speaker and Beauty Queen, UK

"As a woman, do you want to just do a job, or build a career, as these are two completely different things, and although many times we interchange one for the other, it's important for us to recognize what exactly is it you want to do, whether it is earn a salary without much care for promotion, or build a career, implying a strategy of focus, and sacrifices in return." – Kamalika Bose, Urban Conservationist, Founder of Heritage Synergies, India

"Planning is super important. If you really love something, it will come out through the product. I sincerely believe that if you breathe, live, and persist with a passion for your product, it will work out." – Payal Saha, Founder of The Kati Roll Company, New York, USA

"Always trust and believe in yourself. The one thing that will always be a constant in your life is your mind, so take time out to reflect on yourself. It is only when you conquer your mind that you conquer the world," – Ruby Dhillon, Board Member, Pink Attitude Evolution, Toronto, Canada

"Don't lose yourself. As a mother who is always giving and giving, it's easy to forget about yourself and who you are in the process of motherhood. Find ways to keep who you are. Every mom is a good mom, no matter what mistakes you make." – Neesha Desai, CEO of The Chai Mommas, Los Angeles, USA

"…If you have a feeling, trust it. You know your gut feeling is usually correct most of the time so don't undermine yourself and go with it…!" – Reena Dayal, CFO of The Chai Mommas, Los Angeles, USA

"Just surrender. There is no control as a new mom, so just let it be. Be fully in the moment, the ups and the downs. It's such a beautiful, crazy journey so just surrender to it." – Puja Shah, Chief of Content and Strategy, The Chai Mommas, Los Angeles, USA

"Don't give up. You've got this and you're going to be the best mom to the kids that you are blessed to receive. Never stop believing in yourself." – Shraddha Patel, Executive Editor, The Chai Mommas, Los Angeles, USA

"Have a little more faith in yourself and trust your intuition more, as you know more than you give yourself credit for. You face a lot of insecurities, and lack confidence as a new mom, but if you give yourself the benefit of the doubt and aren't so hard on yourself all the time, you may enjoy the journey more. Don't judge your parenting and know that you are doing your best." – Jyoti Chand, Executive Editor, The Chai Mommas, Chicago, USA

"You can do anything you want and can achieve anything you want. All young women should have the belief that they can do anything, and not be bound for what society has set out for you. Do what your heart is telling you to do." – Reshma Patel, Public Office NYC Comptroller Candidate, New York, USA

"Know yourself versus what society and other narratives are telling you. If you have the possibility of knowing your calling, something that really pulls your interests, just go for it! Be able to distinguish a narrative that is for you versus a narrative that you might be hearing from somewhere else." – Sehreen Noorali, Co-Founder of Sleuth, USA

"Hard work is number one. Believe in your dreams, follow your dreams, and especially for younger women entering the construction industry or any industry for that matter, build a strong network of women around you. We take for granted the relationships with mentors that we have bonded with over the years, but that is needed in your journey ahead for advice, opportunities and networking." – Rupila Sethi, Founding Principal, Aerial Design and Build, New York, USA

"Dream big, and never let anyone tell you that you cannot do something. If you follow your dreams, work toward it, then you will achieve it. Dreams can change, but you will succeed if you put your heart and mind to it." – Mariam Mathew, Chief Executive Officer of Manorama Online, Kerala, India

"It's really important to take care of yourself. At the end of the day, if you're not in the best shape possible, it's hard to take care of your loved ones. I would advise journaling or yoga and meditation to help center yourself and give yourself some quiet time. Believe in yourself and dream big. If you don't believe in yourself, how can anyone else do the same for you? Have a plan in place and surround yourself with people who can support you unconditionally." – Sonal Trivedi, Founder and Managing Partner, The COMO Group, Dallas, USA

"Especially in the South Asian culture, we put a lot of emphasis on learning hard skills, doing well in your classes, making sure you have strong math foundations. But it is just as important to invest as much time in learning soft skills, such as negotiations, influence and public speaking. Even if these things come naturally to you, you can always learn from the best. For anyone going into business or looking for inspiration, you can watch shows like this one, The Uma Show, read books, and actually practice negotiating things. Push yourself outside your comfort zone and see how you can practice those skills, because they will always come in handy for life events as well as work." – Anjali Bhatia, Managing Director of North America of Crimson Education, New Jersey, USA

"Just do what you love, what makes you happy, because you are your own boss. And learn to say 'No,' because that simple word can take you to a lot of success and put yourself first, at work, at home, in relationships and beyond." – Shruti Sood, Founder of Morning Lazziness, Madhya Pradesh, India

"Risk is so important, but not just any risk. It has to be a calculated risk on your passion, so you really need to believe and follow your passion. Risk and success go hand in hand, and the biggest risk to your business, is not taking a new risk. If you follow your passion deeply and be truthful to yourself, nothing can stop your path to success." – Tara Bhuyan, Creative Director, Tara Bhuyan Couture, Toronto, Canada

"Patience is key. You cannot solve everything immediately. While it's super important to be motivated and have a goal and a plan, you won't get that job straightaway, or that promotion immediately. You need to put work in, and it does take time to get to things. In reality you will have big jumps in your career, and there will be smaller steps in between that will get you there. Take the time and effort to figure out what gives you the positive energy, even if that is dabbling in different industries." – Era Ray, Co-Founder of SALUTE, New York, USA

"Know your worth. Stop being a people pleaser and putting other people's needs above yours. In Asian societies you are told to be a good girl. No, don't be a good girl, because the definition of that is putting your needs right at the bottom of everyone else's, but the truth is, you are as worthy, if not more, than the next person. Choose who you surround yourself with. There are many people who have negative energy and are naysayers. So choose your friends, boss, and colleagues wisely." – Farzana Baduel, Founder of Curzon PR, London, UK

"Remove self-created barriers, having introspection, and being open to trying new things are all important to knowing where to channel your talents. We are in an age and era where you can achieve anything that you want to, even in what was traditionally known as male roles just by tackling our own self-doubts and working hard at it." – Pallavi Gowda, U.S. Military Veteran, Internal Medicine Doctor, Zumba pro

"When you feel like the odd one out, you are the one that is always trying to fit in, and dress or sound a certain way. But what you should do, is embrace your 'otherness' and your uniqueness, as you have a lot of value to add, and what you say, and think is important to the world. Then, you can really enjoy being who you are, and Be Uma!" – Ruby Kakati Taank, Senior Counsel at Suntory Beverage & Food, London, UK

"You can design a life that you want. You can have both a fulfilling career and a fulfilling family, so don't let anybody tell you that you cannot do it. There is always a way, and as long as you follow your passions and you stick with your core values, you will be able to do those things... Also, pursuing a medical career is a long journey, so don't sweat the small stuff." – Pamela Mehta, Board certified Orthopedic Surgeon, San Jose, USA

"Pick one thing that you really care about, then don't just learn about it but do something about it. Find ways to get involved and make a change." – Aditi Juneja, Organizer, Lawyer and Writer, New York, USA

"If you really want to be in a particular profession, create a niche and a specialized form of what you are skilled at. Even though your world may not be that large, you are the expert in it and not competing with others. Use your special skill as the mission to change people's minds." – Sunita Bhuyan Khaund, Indofusion Musician and Leadership Trainer, Mumbai, India

**Advice from our Uma Ambassadors**
"I always believe that it is much better to be great at a few things, rather than being 'just OK' in a lot of things, and whatever you do choose to do, always put in one hundred percent effort, otherwise don't do it." – Asma Rabbani, Uma Ambassador, San Francisco, USA

"A dream becomes reality when you put it in writing. Dream big and don't let anyone tell you it can't be done. If they tell you it can't be done, prove them wrong!" – Elizabeth Koraca, Uma Ambassador, Los Angeles, USA

"Finding balance looks very different at different stages in your work and life journey. Finding the type of people and environment that motivates you is the common thread at every stage." – Rima Roy, Uma Ambassador, New York, USA

"It's important to own your story and show others what's possible. It took me a long time to be comfortable with sharing my background—where I come from and what I believe in. But over time I have learned that there's strength in authenticity. I have learned to be unapologetically myself, to not be afraid if I am the only one who looks or speaks like me in a room. The world is going to pay attention and overcome its biases, one person at a time." – Shajia Meraj, Uma Ambassador, London, UK

"To all the mothers, wives, and daughters looking to get back into the workforce, don't let the sacrifices of yesterday come in the way of your tomorrow. Keep shaping the future for your kids and being a role model to them. Use your inner strength to navigate your path ahead, as you are strong, and can achieve both your career and family goals. Go forth with passion, purpose, and confidence, and make a difference in the world!" – Vaishnavi Venugopal, Uma Ambassador, New York, USA

**Inspiration from Team Uma around the world**
"As women and people of minority backgrounds, it is up to us to raise our voices, and speak up not only for ourselves, but to lift each other up too. As changemakers our goal should not only be to survive, but to thrive and continue to push barriers. Only then can we move ahead and redefine stereotypes." – Valentina Dangond, Team Uma, Barranquilla, Colombia

"Your biggest source of confidence and inspiration will come from your family. You will see ups and downs in your career and life but your family, your support system, will be there for you. As a mother, developer and entrepreneur, my most powerful driving force is my two daughters. For them to look up to me as they grow up and be proud of their own dreams, they first need to see me as an independent, confident and strong woman, and someone they can aspire to follow." – Upola Gogoi Gohain, IT Specialist, Team Uma, Chennai, India

"Careers for working mums are ever evolving. There's no such thing as one career path anymore, so you need to have flexibility and adapt with your life changes. Companies are also recognizing the need to adapt, which we have seen more than ever during the pandemic, which has showcased how flexible working arrangements actually can work, for all genders." – Andri Paphitis, UK Operations, Team Uma, London, UK

"Energy is our internal life source. Our energy goes to where we focus and what we think. Always think positively and look for solutions rather than dwelling into problems. In order to reach your goals, first find what you love, and then remove all extra energy drains in your life such as negative thoughts, people, doubts, unnecessary tasks, etc., and put all your efforts into your goal." – Ecem Bellikci, Team Uma, London, UK

"A lesson my parents taught me is that forming relationships, both on a personal and professional level, will give you the most inspiration and make the greatest impact throughout your life. To paint the picture during the past year, I was led to the concept of Maraasim, a place where residents of senior care homes can connect with children in foster care homes, and there was nothing more powerful than to see the strength of connection and bonding again." – Manya Gupta, Team Uma, London, UK

"We are told to be humble way too often and that showing what we are good at looks bad 'on a woman.' But we need to change that way of thinking. Be kind to yourself, congratulate yourself when you do a good job, celebrate yourself when you achieve your goals. Be proud of your journey and how far you've come, then others will see it too." – Romina Renjifo Lozano, Team Uma, London, UK

"Resilience and the willingness to learn enable you to face adversity courageously and to thrive in spite of it. By being an optimist you empower yourself to find creative solutions and inspire others." – Soyan Daniel, Team Uma, London, UK

"To truly succeed, we must not only persist and work exceptionally hard, but also come together as an inclusive community and help one another to progress, which is something Uma has been both advocating for and executing since its formation." – Tereza Fedorova, Team Uma, London, UK

"As women, we are continuously juggling being a mom, sister, wife, partner, friend, and having a career at the same time! Sometimes we get caught up in all the labels of who we are supposed to be and forget that just being is okay." – Sammy D'Ambrosio, Team Uma, Los Angeles, USA

"There is no specific recipe for success. You simply sprinkle ingredients of what you love to do, what you consider important, or what you're passionate about. You throw it all into a pot or pan and top it with patience and consistency. Your success is your own creation." – Elizabeth Kim, Team Uma, Los Angeles, USA

"Every failure is one step toward success. Don't just dwell on your mistakes... learn from them! After all, you just need that *one* acceptance to make you forget about the hundreds of prior rejections. Remember, that the worst thing a person you reached out to can say to you is 'No'. So, build and utilize your network! Ultimately, don't lose sight of your goals, because at the end of the day, you are the only person that will hold yourself accountable." – Jun Ishida, Team Uma, Los Angeles, USA

"Treat failures and setbacks as a sign you're doing something right; because if you aren't challenging yourself with something new and worthwhile, you will never get to experience failure." – Angela Wang, Team Uma, Los Angeles, USA

"Appreciate your differences. Our differences hold the keys to big achievements, success and true happiness." – Tasha Ro, Creative Lead, Team Uma, New York, USA

"Believe in yourself, your success, dreams and passion. Because if you don't, then no one else will either." – Dhvani Mehta, Team Uma, New York, USA

"While the business world is busy with increasing their diversification efforts for women, Uma is a step ahead by investing in inclusion for women in order to help build a sustainable and successful culture for such organizations." – Anmol Sachdeva, Team Uma, New York, USA

"Believe that you have the potential to change, to break away from any current unsatisfactory status into someone very different. What may have happened to you in the past doesn't define who you are now. It's your decision and conscious choice to make you who you are going to be. Be sure to have a growth mindset, and not a fixed one." – Yarui Peng, Team Uma, New York, USA

"Psychology and life has taught me that a powerful, successful woman is only frightening to those who are weaker and incompetent!" – Trish McLernon, Team Uma, New York, USA

"When I wake up feeling down, like there are clouds all around, then I take a deep breath, smile and dream of an image or memory of something that makes me feel happy and positive again. A memory that drives and motivates me to feel much better. It is so important to find a moment within ourselves and to remember that after the rain there is always sunshine." – Ada Criado, Latin American Operations, Team Uma, Puerto Rico, USA

"It's always important to remember that every setback is merely a new learning opportunity." – Diksha Mehta, Team Uma, Toronto, Canada

"For anyone who finds themselves back in the job market with or without experience or is a new immigrant or rejoining the workforce after a gap, remember that job searching and building a career is a journey that continues even after you get an offer. Also, it's normal for your confidence level to fluctuate, so be sure to celebrate the positives, rather than focus solely on development points. Finding and succeeding in a job is a team effort, so take the time to acknowledge those who helped in your journey, whether it was a mentor, manager, or colleague who offered you some water or a cup of coffee. Lastly, don't forget to practice, practice, and practice to be that best version of yourself!" – Kavyashi Duttabaruah Mahanta, Team Uma, Toronto, Canada

# Uma-isms

*"Take a stand. Be known for your courage and confidence."*
*– Indra Nooyi*

Here are some popular Uma terms we typically use in our workshops and training sessions:

Allyship: A journey of ongoing commitment between a person with privilege and/or power and a person from a minority group, to share experiences, build trust, champion for and take action for change.

Be Yourself: The key to your soul, where a future of confidence, empowerment, and freedom awaits.

Building Trust: Built over time with honesty, integrity and clear communication, social interaction and set expectations.

Confidence: The unshakable desire to Be Bold. Be You. Be Uma.

Communications: The secret sauce to conveying information with clarity, concision and confidence.

Conflict Resolution: The art of reaching mutual understanding by clear and structured communication.

Decency: The genuine desire to do right by others.

Differences: A celebration of your personality, quirks, and talents, all which make you unique.

Diversity: The many rich cultural heritages, cuisines, languages, appearances, abilities, and genders that exist within your communities.

Empowerment: The ability to unleash your inner goddess of go-getting through listening, empathy, and deliberation.

Failure: The foundation for reflection, acceptance, resilience, and ultimately the building blocks for success.

Goddess of Go-Getting: Unleash the inner voice inside of you. Be Bold. Be You. Be Uma.

Impostor Syndrome: When feelings of not belonging, inferiority and not being deserving of achievements, engulf you.

Inclusion: An environment where the many different communities along with their rich cultural heritages can all feel welcome and like they belong.

Inner Voice: Your hidden superpower to speak up. Be Bold. Be You. Be Uma.

International Women's Day: March 8th is the annual day to celebrate the Uma inside all of us.

Kindness: An impact like no other. Kindness is contagious, uplifting and spreads positive vibes all around.

Love Yourself: The ultimate route to becoming a goddess of go-getting through self-belief, respect and loving yourself!

Mentorship: A relationship of unconditional encouragement, support and positive guidance.

Negotiation: An art form that requires preparation, practice, and precision to unleash the power of persuasion inside of you!

Problem Solving: The ability to identify the root cause of issues and offer creative solutions calmly and with flexibility.

Reach for the Stars: The act of pursuing your dreams, through confidence, empowerment, and resilience.

Reliability: Being known as honest, communicative, trustworthy, and for timely delivery, consistently.

Resolutions: New start. New beginnings. How to make and stick with your goals.

Roadmapping: Strategies for navigating your career path to success!

Role Model: Someone you can see in order to be.

Rules of the Playground: The key to your future likeability stems from your ability to know when to play tag, share the slide, pass the basketball, or give up the swing.

Saying No: A life skill. The ability to comfortably push back, delegate, or politely decline.

Success: The mindset of grit, perseverance, passion and adaptability to achieve milestones and goals that are important to you and set by you.

Uma: A Hindu Goddess, who is a mother, daughter, sibling and wife. She is strong, determined and full of courage. She is truly the goddess of go-getting!

Unwind: It's time to switch off, relax your mind, and take a break.

Workplace Culture: Shared values, beliefs, attitudes and ethos that you can "feel" in the workplace.

# Endnotes

[1] "Executive Summary, State of Workplace Empathy, 2019" by Business Solver; 2019; https://cdn2.hubspot.net/hubfs/378546/ empathy-2019/2019%20Empathy%20Exec%20Summary/ businessolver-2019-workplace-empathy-executive-summary.pdf? __hssc=244580634.3.1571088112946&__hstc=244580634.9f0c 8e73da0302600568c97b632973ec.1571088112945.1571088112945. 1571088112945.1&__hsfp=1060679430&hsCtaTracking=184e6df9 -5773-4123-8822-6f5df646b551%7Cef554b97-ba28-4f64-8a4b- ff8092126d49

[2] "Why It Pays to Invest in Gender Diversity" by Morgan Stanley; Research Report; May 11, 2016; https://www.morganstanley.com/ideas/ gender-diversity-investment-framework

[3] "2019 Workplace Happiness Report" by Udemy; Udemy Snapshot; 2019; https://research.udemy.com/ wp-content/uploads/2019/05/Udemy_2019_Workplace_Happiness _Exec_Summary_FINAL-1.pdf

[4] "Women in the Workplace 2021" by LeanIn.Org and McKinsey & Company; LeanIn.Org report authors and contributors: Ali Bohrer, Jenna Bott, Gina Cardazone, Marianne Cooper, Destin Fernandes, Sophia Hunt, Ryan Hutson, Sonia Mahajan, Jordan Miller-Surratt, Mary Noble-Tolla, Rachel Thomas, Emma Tsurkov, Kate Urban, Katie Wullert, Jemma York; McKinsey & Company report authors and contributors: Sofia Alvarado, Tiffany Burns, David Corfield, Nawel Gabouge, Worth Gentry, Alison Gerard, Beatriz Go, Sanchika Gupta, Anne Marie Hawley, Jess Huang, Alexis Krivkovich, Melinda Lee, Yuan Qu, Ishanaa Rambachan,

Tijana Trkulja, Lareina Yee, Stephanie Yeh, Zhengren Zhu; https://womenintheworkplace.com/#about

[5] "You And Your Business Have 7 Seconds To Make A First Impression: Here's How To Succeed" by Serenity Gibbons; Forbes; June 19, 2018; https://www.forbes.com/sites/serenitygibbons/2018/06/19/you-have-7-seconds-to-make-a-first-impression-heres-how-to-succeed/?sh=10bbe1d556c2

[6] "Biography of Ada Lovelace, First Computer Programmer" by Robert Longley; ThoughtCo.; February 19, 2021; https://www.thoughtco.com/ada-lovelace-biography-5113321#:~:text=Ada%20Lovelace%20%28born%20Augusta%20Ada%20Byron%3B%20December%2010%2C,computing%20machine%20built%20by%20Charles%20Babbage%20in%201821.

[7] "Shirley Jackson at MIT, 1973" by MIT Black History; https://www.blackhistory.mit.edu/archive/shirley-jackson-mit-1973

[8] "Katherine Johnson Biography" by Margot Lee Shetterly; https://www.nasa.gov/content/katherine-johnson-biography

[9] "Rosalind Franklin, Biophysicist" by King's College London; Biography; https://www.kcl.ac.uk/people/rosalind-franklin

[10] Parenthood and Productivity of Highly Skilled Labor: Evidence from the Groves of Academe" by Matthias Krapf, Heinrich W. Ursprung, Christian Zimmermann; January 2014; https://s3.amazonaws.com/real.stlouisfed.org/wp/2014/2014-001.pdf; https://doi.org/10.20955/wp.2014.001

[11] "Women in the Workplace 2021" by LeanIn.Org and McKinsey & Company;

LeanIn.Org report authors and contributors:
Ali Bohrer, Jenna Bott, Gina Cardazone, Marianne Cooper,
Destin Fernandes, Sophia Hunt, Ryan Hutson, Sonia Mahajan,
Jordan Miller-Surratt, Mary Noble-Tolla, Rachel Thomas,
Emma Tsurkov, Kate Urban, Katie Wullert, and Jemma York;
McKinsey & Company report authors and contributors:
Sofia Alvarado, Tiffany Burns, David Corfield, Nawel Gabouge,
Worth Gentry, Alison Gerard, Beatriz Go, Sanchika Gupta,
Anne Marie Hawley, Jess Huang, Alexis Krivkovich,
Melinda Lee, Yuan Qu, Ishanaa Rambachan, Tijana Trkulja,
Lareina Yee, Stephanie Yeh, and Zhengren Zhu;
https://womenintheworkplace.com/#about

[12] Stay-at-Home Moms Are Half as Likely to Get a Job Interview
as Moms Who Got Laid Off" by Kate Weisshaar; Harvard
Business Review; February 22, 2018;
https://hbr.org/2018/02/stay-at-home-moms-are-half-as-likely-
to-get-a-job-interview-as-moms-who-got-laid-off

[13] "Flex Time Flourishes in Accounting Industry"
by Steven Greenhouse; *The New York Times*; Jan 7, 2012;
https://www.nytimes.com/2011/01/08/business/08perks.html?_r=2;

[14] "It's Time to Kill the 9 to 5"
by Rebecca Greenfield; Bloomberg; September 19, 2017;
https://www.bloomberg.com/news/articles/2016-09-19/
it-s-time-to-kill-the-9-to-5

[15] "The Employment Situation"
by Bureau of Labor and Statistics; News Release;
U.S. Department of Labor;
https://www.bls.gov/news.release/pdf/empsit.pdf

[16] "Why People Really Quit Their Jobs,"
By Lori Goler, Janelle Gale, Brynn Harrington, and Adam Grant;
Harvard Business Review; January 11, 2018;
https://hbr.org/2018/01/why-people-really-quit-their-jobs

[17] "The Biggest Cost of Doing Business:
A Closer Look at Labor Costs" by Paycor; December 24, 2020;
https://www.paycor.com/resource-center/articles/
the-biggest-cost-of-doing-business-a-closer-look-at-labor-costs/
#:~:text=Labor%20costs%2C%20which%20can%20account%20
for%20as%20much,spend%2015%25%20of%20their%20
time%20managing%20labor%20costs.

[18] "Cost of Employee Turnover vs Retention Proposition"
by Anna Verasai; The HR Digest; March 16, 2018;
https://www.thehrdigest.com/cost-of-employee-turnover-vs-
retention-proposition/

[19] "Deloitte finds millennials' confidence in business takes a
sharp turn; they feel unprepared for Industry 4.0"
by Deloitte; May 15, 2018;
https://en.prnasia.com/releases/apac/deloitte-finds-millennials-
confidence-in-business-takes-a-sharp-turn-they-feel-
unprepared-for-industry-4-0-210863.shtml

[20] "Survey: Flexibility, wellness key to employee retention"
by Marlene Satter, Benefits Pro; February 14, 2019;
https://www.benefitspro.com/2019/02/14/survey-flexibility-
wellness-key-to-employee-retention/?kw=Survey:%20
Flexibility%2C%20wellness%20key%20to%20employee%20
retention&utm_source=email&utm_medium=enl&
utm_campaign=bprodaily&utm_content=20190215&
utm_term=bpro&slreturn=20190829185128

[21] "Types of Discrimination in the Workplace"
by Alison Doyle; The Balance Careers; June 23, 2020;
https://www.thebalancecareers.com/types-of-employment-
discrimination-with-examples-2060914

[22] "Maslow's Hierarchy of Needs"
by Dr. Saul McLeod; Simply Psychology; December 29, 2020;
https://www.simplypsychology.org/maslow.html

23 Hertzberg's Motivation-Hygiene Theory: Two-factor"
by Dr. Serhat Kurt; Education Library; March 31, 2021;
https://educationlibrary.org/herzbergs-motivation-hygiene-
theory-two-factor/

24 "The Big Three of Workplace Success: Differences,
Diversity and Decency"
by Rita Kakati-Shah; P.149; Women in Business,
Mission Matters; November 2020;
https://www.amazon.com/Rita-Kakati-Shah/e/B08N363GB6/
ref=ntt_dp_epwbk_1

25 "How To Teach Empathy"
by Terry Heick; Teach Thought;
https://www.teachthought.com/pedagogy/how-to-teach-empathy/

26 "Access to Capital for Women- and Minority-owned Businesses:
Revisiting Key Variables"
by Christine Kymn; SBA Office of Advocacy; January 29, 2014;
https://www.sba.gov/sites/default/files/Issue%20Brief%203%20
Access%20to%20Capital.pdf

27 "Women in the Workplace 2021"
by Tiffany Burns, Jess Huang, Alexis Krivkovich, Lareina Yee,
Ishanaa Rambachan, and Tijana Trkulja; McKinsey & Company;
September 27, 2021;
https://www.mckinsey.com/featured-insights/diversity-
and-inclusion/women-in-the-workplace

28 "The 2019 State of Workplace Empathy Study:
The Competitive Edge Leaders are Missing"
by Rae Shanahan; Businesssolver; March 28, 2019;
https://blog.businesssolver.com/the-2019-state-of-workplace-
empathy-study-the-competitive-edge-leaders-are-missing#gref

29 "The State of Workplace Empathy, 2021 State of Workplace
Empathy," Businesssolver; 2021;

https://www.businessolver.com/resources/businessolver-empathy-monitor?utm_source=WashPO&utm_campaign=rewards%20multiply&utm_medium=rich%20media%20article

[30] "Why Employees Need Both Recognition and Appreciation" by Mike Robbins, Harvard Business Review, November 12, 2019; https://hbr.org/2019/11/why-employees-need-both-recognition-and-appreciation

[31] "Businessolver Finds Workplaces Still Lack Empathy," Businesssolver; May 18, 2017; https://www.businessolver.com/who-we-are/news/businessolver-finds-workplaces-still-lack-empathy#gref

[32] "The Annual IWG Global Workspace Survey: Welcome To Generation Flex – The Employee Power Shif," by International Workplace Group; 2019; http://www.iwgplc.com/global-workspace-survey-2019

[33] "New Research Shows That Flexible Working is Now a Top Consideration in the War for Talent" by International Workplace Group; March 27, 2019; https://www.prnewswire.com/news-releases/new-research-shows-that-flexible-working-is-now-a-top-consideration-in-the-war-for-talent-300818790.html?tc=eml_cleartime

[34] "Survey: Flexibility, wellness key to employee retention" by Marlene Satter; Benefits Pro; February 14, 2019; https://www.benefitspro.com/2019/02/14/survey-flexibility-wellness-key-to-employee-retention/?kw=Survey:%20Flexibility%2C%20wellness%20key%20to%20employee%20retention&utm_source=email&utm_medium=enl&utm_campaign=bprodaily&utm_content=20190215&utm_term=bpro

[35] "Employee Retention: What You Need to Know (Part I)" by Melissa Asher; ELGL; January 15, 2019; https://elgl.org/employee-retention-what-you-need-to-know/

[36] http://www.oracle.com/us/products/applications/talent-magnet-3236631.pdf

[37] "Exploring the Impact of the Skills Gap and
Employment-Based Immigration"
by Society of Human Resources Management (SHRM);
2019 State of the Workplace;
https://www.shrm.org/about-shrm/Documents/SHRM%20
State%20of%20Workplace_Bridging%20the%20Talent%20
Gap.pdf

[38] "You And Your Business Have 7 Seconds To Make A
First Impression: Here's How To Succeed"
by Serenity Gibbons; Forbes; June 19, 2018;
https://www.forbes.com/sites/serenitygibbons/2018/06/19/
you-have-7-seconds-to-make-a-first-impression-heres-how-to-
succeed/?sh=10bbe1d556c2

[39] "Why Companies Have Started to Coach New Parents"
by Tara Siegel Bernard; *The New York Times*;

July 22, 2016; https://www.nytimes.com/2016/07/23/your-money/
why-companies-have-started-to-coach-new-parents.html

[40] "Family Supportive Supervisor Behaviors (FSSB) Training
Manual" by Leslie Hammer and Ellen Kossek; Based on the FSSB
training used with managers/supervisors as part of the STAR and
START initiative; October, 2013;
https://projects.iq.harvard.edu/files/wfhn/files/fssb_training_
manual10_13.pdf

[41] "THE IWG GLOBAL WORKSPACE SURVEY,
Welcome to Generation Flex – the employee power shift"
by International Workplace Group; March, 2019;
http://assets.regus.com/pdfs/iwg-workplace-survey/iwg-workplace-
survey-2019.pdf

[42] "How Puberty Kills Girls' Confidence"
by Claire Shipman, Katty Kay, and JillEllyn Riley; *The Atlantic*;
September 20, 2018;
https://www.theatlantic.com/family/archive/2018/09/puberty-girls-confidence/563804/

[43] "You And Your Business Have 7 Seconds To Make A
First Impression: Here's How To Succeed"
by Serenity Gibbons; Forbes; June 19, 2018;
https://www.forbes.com/sites/serenitygibbons/2018/06/19/you-have-7-seconds-to-make-a-first-impression-heres-how-to-succeed/?sh=10bbe1d556c2

[44] "'Good-looking' pupils perform better in school, research
finds" by Christopher Ingraham; Independent;

November 3, 2019; https://www.independent.co.uk/news/education/pupils-school-good-looking-attractive-education-study-a9183111.html

[45] "One type of diversity we don't talk about at work: body size"
by Julia Carpenter; CNN Business; January 3, 2019;
https://www.cnn.com/2019/01/03/success/weight-bias-work/index.html

[46] "Your body language may shape who you are"
by Dr. Amy Cuddy; TED Talk; October 1, 2021;
https://www.bing.com/videos/search?q=amy+cuddy+power+pose&docid=608008386754906847&mid=586E6DB114506CCF5D1D586E6DB114506CCF5D1D&view=detail&FORM=VIRE

[47] "You And Your Business Have 7 Seconds To Make A
First Impression: Here's How To Succeed" by Serenity Gibbons;
Forbes; June 19, 2018;
https://www.forbes.com/sites/serenitygibbons/2018/06/19/you-have-7-seconds-to-make-a-first-impression-heres-how-to-succeed/?sh=10bbe1d556c2

[48] "How Many Seconds to a First Impression?"
by Eric Wargo; Association for Psychological Science;
July 1, 2006;
https://www.psychologicalscience.org/observer/how-many-seconds-to-a-first-impression

[49] "Finland's Women-Led Government Has Equalized
Family Leave: 7 Months For Each Parent"
by Laurel Wamsley; NPR; February 5, 2020;
https://www.npr.org/2020/02/05/803051237/finlands-women-led-government-has-equalized-family-leave-7-months-for-each-paren?utm_term=nprnews&utm_campaign=npr&utm_medium=social&utm_source=facebook.com

[50] "Half of Brits think there are more advantages to
being a man than a woman"
by Ipsos MORI, the Global Institute of Women's
Leadership at King's College London, and International
Women's Day; March 5, 2019;
https://www.ipsos.com/ipsos-mori/en-uk/international-womens-day-2019

[51] "Pygmalion effect," Wikipedia.org;
https://en.wikipedia.org/wiki/Pygmalion_effect

[52] "The Secrets to Living a Longer and Better Life"
by Jeffrey Kluger and Alexandra Sifferlin; Time;
February 15, 2018;
https://time.com/5159852/the-surprising-secrets-to-living-longer-and-better/

[53] Gender Inequality Costs as Much as the American and
Chinese Economies Combined"
by Charlotte Alter; *Time,* September 24, 2015;
https://time.com/4045115/gender-inequality-economy/

[54] "Half of Brits think there are more advantages to being a man than a woman" by Ipsos MORI, the Global Institute of Women's Leadership at King's College London, and International Women's Day; March 5, 2019; https://www.ipsos.com/ipsos-mori/en-uk/international-womens-day-2019

[55] "Why closing Japan's gender gap will be achieved with equality from the top," World Economic Forum (weforum.org); March 30, 2021; https://www.weforum.org/agenda/2021/03/japan-gender-gap-political-leadership/

RITA KAKATI-SHAH is an award-winning, gender, diversity, inclusion and career strategist, speaker, author and advisor to Fortune 500 companies. She is the Founder and CEO of Uma, an international diversity and inclusion strategic advisory, coaching, consulting, and corporate training platform that empowers confidence, inspires success, and builds leadership and resilience in women and minorities around the world. Prior to Uma, Rita lead Business Development globally in CNS healthcare. Rita began her professional career at Goldman Sachs in London, where she was awarded the prestigious Excellence in Citizenship and Diversity Award. She is also a Distinguished Alumna of King's College London and a three-time Stevie Awards for Women in Business winner, and judge for the Middle East Awards. Rita is also an honoree of the President's Lifetime Achievement Award from US President Joe Biden, as well as recipient of several international awards in recognition of advancing gender equality, diversity and inclusion, and empowering women, girls and youth around the world.

Rita is a graduate of King's Business School, now serving on its Advisory Council, and is actively involved with the King's College London Leadership, Diversity and Entrepreneurial Institute Mentoring Programs, as well as being part of the New York and Los Angeles Alumni Committees. Rita is also affiliated with University of Southern California, where she speaks, teaches, and mentors students. Rita also actively coaches and mentors business leaders, military veterans, survivors of domestic violence, women in technology/STEM, schoolgirls, students and entrepreneurs. She also serves as an advisor, ambassador, and diversity and inclusion expert to multiple boards, advisory councils, academic institutions, and global organizations around the world, spanning multiple disciplines and sectors.

Rita is a recognized thought leader, keynote speaker and guest lecturer on gender equality, diversity and inclusion, at various academic institutions, multinational corporations and global policy forums such as UNESCO in Paris, European Parliament in Brussels, and many more spanning Assam, Delhi, Hyderabad, Kolkata, London, Madrid, Meghalaya, Moscow, Mumbai, Nairobi, New York, Sambalpur, San Francisco, Sirmaur, Sochi, Toronto and Zambia, where she uniquely focuses on confidence, communication and culture. Some of the academic institutions where Rita has taught include USC Marshall School of Business, London Business School, New York University Steinhardt, Baruch College CUNY, Stanley Engineering College for Women in Hyderabad, Gauhati University, Nowgong Girls' College, and several Indian Institutes of Management across India.

Rita has been featured as an expert on multiple international television and news shows, interviewed and quoted in various podcasts and publications such as *The Wall Street Journal, Fast Company, Entrepreneur, Fortune, Thrive Global, Dell Technology, CBS News, Fox News, Yahoo Finance, LA Weekly* and *iHeartRadio*. She also hosts the popular South Asian television show, *The Uma Show*, on *Mana TV International*. Rita has also co-authored books on women in business, diversity and inclusion, and is also a trained classical Indian dancer in the forms of Bharata Natyam and Xattriya, enjoys post-Impressionist oil painting, is a foodie, and loves trying new spots for afternoon tea around New York City, where she lives with her husband, two children and puppy.

We hope you enjoyed reading *The Goddess of Go-Getting*, and welcome you to write a review!

To book Rita for speaking engagements, trainings, strategic consulting and coaching, or to get in touch with Rita's team, contact Uma at beboldbeuma.com or email pr@beboldbeuma.com.

Follow Uma @BeBoldBeUma on Twitter, Instagram, Facebook, and BeBoldBeUma on YouTube.

Follow @RitaKakatiShah on Twitter, rita.kakati on Instagram, Rita Kakati-Shah on LinkedIn, and visit Rita's author page at ritakakatishah.com to stay in touch.

CPSIA information can be obtained
at www.ICGtesting.com
Printed in the USA
LVHW101304050522
718022LV00008B/18/J